El Norte

El Norte

THE · CUISINE · OF
NORTHERN · MEXICO

James W. Peyton

R·E·D
CRANE
BOOKS

First Edition

Printed in the United States of America

Photographs by James W. Peyton
Illustrations by Andrea Peyton
Cover and text design by Kathleen Katz

Library of Congress Cataloging-in-Publication Data
Peyton, James W.
    El Norte: The Cuisine of Northern Mexico
    Includes index.
    ISBN 1-878610-04-X

Red Crane Books
826 Camino de Monte Rey
Santa Fe, New Mexico 87501

DEDICATION

It is only fitting that this book be dedicated to the people of
northern Mexico who have provided so much joy. We have a great
deal more to learn from them about living than just their recipes.

CONTENTS

PREFACE

Northern Mexico is ranch country. There the good land is grazing land, and cowboys and horses work a space that goes purple at the edge. Most of the cooking is still done over an open fire.

It is the pervasiveness of the campfire, I believe, which gives the cooking of this region its uniqueness and adds to the food a subtle flavor of the wild.

This love of a wood fire is common from back country to *hacienda*, where the cooking for traditional weekend *fiestas* is always done on the ground outdoors. Meals are prepared over wood fires in the villages, where few homes are without a patio and a woodburning oven. In the cities, too, most restaurants prepare mesquite-smoked meat over grills.

What in the United States is generally thought of as "Mexican food" is really *antojitos* or snacks from the south of Mexico—*tacos, enchiladas, tamales* and the like. Several excellent cookbooks have introduced us, also, to the more elaborate and complexly sauced dishes of that region.

But the cuisine of Northern Mexico, too, is beginning to find a following north of the Border. Recently, the popularity of such mesquite-grilled dishes as *fajitas* has spread from the Southwest. In fact, there are probably few cities in this country where *fajitas* are not featured now on restaurant menus. This book celebrates the cuisine of the north, the "other" Mexico. On these pages the reader will find a comprehensive array of dishes from a style of cooking which favors broiling and beef and flour *tortillas*, and a perhaps unexpected variety of seafood entrees. Familiarity with the many subtleties of this cuisine, some of which found their way to the open range through immigrant sheepherders from the Basque region of Spain, is sure to enhance the pleasures of your table.

One of the happy surprises for the reader is that this fare, for all its variety and distinction, is amazingly easy to prepare, using ingredients that are readily available. Surely this simplicity is born of the campfire tradition, of dwindling daylight that calls for shortcuts, and saddlebags that admit no more than the most essential ingredients and tools.

The recipes of this book are the foods of the open fire, a flavor of burning mesquite that blends with the evening breeze: the cuisine of *El Norte*.

ACKNOWLEDGMENTS

One of the things you learn from writing a book requiring research over an extended period is that you should keep a detailed record of all those who help. After more than sixteen years of work on the project there is no way that I can remember all those who provided assistance, much less find the space to thank them. Many were cooks in restaurants and many more supplied food at private gatherings. So, I have decided to confine my expressions of gratitude to those whose contributions were critical. I hope the countless others who shared their cooking and helped in so many ways will realize how much I appreciate their efforts. My sincere thanks to them and to the following:

My wife Andrea whose love, support and patience have been complete and unselfish. My mother who instilled in me the love of travel and adventure, "a double edged sword." Andy Martin and Charles Busch who were there during the early research and helped with the writing. Ray Salcido for his olives, *salsa*, fabulous memories, and so much else that helped. Truman Smith who shared his home and friendships, and without whom my understanding of Mexico would not have been possible. All the fine people at Red Crane Books and especially Jim Mafchir and Harriet Slavitz: Jim for his confidence and guidance, and Harriet for her expertise and kindness in helping a new author through the process. Also, Kathleen Katz for her fine contribution in the design of this book, and Winnie Culp for her help. Jose Ortega, a true scholar, who provided both encouragement and help with the Spanish. Ralph Howell, a fine photographer and teacher, whose advice and many hours in the darkroom made the photographs possible. David Cohen, owner of the marvelous Old Mexico Grill, in Santa Fe, New Mexico, for his encouragement and review of the manuscript. Dave Dewitt of the *Whole Chile Pepper Magazine* for his suggestions and help in clearing up some of the more confusing issues in the section on *chiles*. Rogelio Chavarría whose hospitality and friendship would make anyone feel a part of northern Mexico. Gabriel and Elena Renero who, among other things, went to a great deal of trouble to deliver a *tortilladora*. Margo Given for her typing in the early days. Johnny

Rodriquéz whose knowledge of Chihuahua helped enormously. Juan Elguezabel for showing me how to make *asadero* cheese. Polo Elguezabel for the information on making *machaca* and the tour of the "Kickapoo" dried beef factory. Rudy and Pat Lira and Margarita Abril of Tania's Flour Tortillas and Mexican Food in Tucson, Arizona, for spending a morning revealing the secrets of making Sonora style *tortillas*.

El Norte

STATES OF
NORTHERN MEXICO

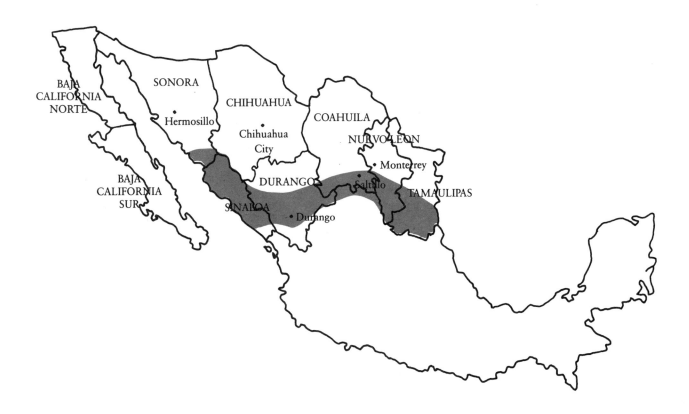

BAJA CALIFORNIA NORTE

SONORA

Hermosillo

CHIHUAHUA

Chihuahua City

COAHUILA

NUEVO LEON

Monterrey

BAJA CALIFORNIA SUR

DURANGO

Saltillo

SINALOA

Durango

TAMAULIPAS

NORTH   -   *Upper blank area*
TRANSITIONAL   -   *Shaded area*
SOUTH   -   *Lower blank area*

INTRODUCTION

When you cross the Border into northern Mexico, the sweet smoky tang of meat cooking over mesquite, mingled with the pungency of garlic, onions and *chiles*, instantly invites the senses. Whether prepared in sun-baked adobe ovens, over campfires or in elaborate commercial kitchens, this distinctive cuisine recently has begun to inspire the more venturesome chefs of the United States.

That cooking reflects culture is nowhere more evident than in Mexico. Before the arrival of the Conquistadors, the Indians of both north and south lived on a limited diet of corn, beans and game flavored with *chiles*. With the Spanish came greater variety: pork, beef, lamb, wheat, sugar, cheese, garlic, vinegar and limes. The combined resources of both cultures created the cuisines of Mexico as we know them today. In the south, where cooking evolved from ancient Indian recipes modified by the Spanish, the ingredients were those of the traditional small farm economy and much of the cooking was done in clay ovens. The cooking of northern Mexico, on the other hand, was developed by and for the *vaqueros*, sheepherders, landowners, banished intellectuals and smugglers who settled the frontier.

The people of northern Mexico brought recipes from their many places of origin and adapted them to the available ingredients. Over the years the recipes merged, as did the people, creating a distinctive cooking tradition. Newcomers were drawn to northern Mexico because of the adventure and opportunities offered by the frontier. Sheepherders from the Basque area of Spain brought their cooking techniques, garlic and olive oil, and immigrants from southern Mexico brought their corn-based dishes and *tortillas*. *Vaqueros* from both sides of the Border created the outdoor broiling techniques so well suited to beef dishes and the nomadic nature of ranch life. As time went on, talented chefs adapted local ingredients to recipes learned elsewhere: garlic soup and garlic sauce from Spain; shishkebob from the Middle East; from Italy a dish called *milanesa*, a breaded and fried veal or tenderloin; and *antojitos* from the south of Mexico. Each dish, altered to suit the northern taste and ingredients, became unique in the process.

1

Southern Mexico is renowned for its complex sauces which complement the usually oven-baked or braised chicken, pork, seafood and corn–based dishes, commonly served with corn *tortillas*. The northern cuisine, however, is based on beef, lamb and *cabrito* (kid) cooked over mesquite wood or charcoal, and served with flour *tortillas* as often as corn. *Fajitas*, charbroiled strips of skirt steak, a dish currently enjoying great popularity in the United States, is probably the best known example of the cooking of northern Mexico.

While meats are the staple in northern Mexico, seafood also plays an important part in the cuisine. Elegant waiters hurrying by with plates of broiled black bass brought in daily from Boquillas Reservoir are a common sight in Ciudad Juárez's fine restaurants. In Guaymas you will find huge platters of broiled and fried shrimp. The fishing village of Puerto Nuevo, located between Tijuana and Ensenada, specializes in a unique lobster dish served with beans, rice, hot sauce and huge, paper thin flour *tortillas*.

However, it is not only ingredients and cooking methods that distinguish northern from southern cooking, but also the distinctive combinations of foods and the sauces with which the food is served. A Filet Tampiqueña (the ultimate Mexican combination plate) served at the México Típico restaurant in Nuevo Laredo best illustrates this. In addition to charbroiled strips of tenderloin, the plate includes a chicken *enchilada* in *mole* sauce, a crisp chicken *taco*, refried beans, Mexican rice, *rajas* (strips of fried *chile poblano* and onion), chunks of fried potatoes, *guacamole* and a garnish of sliced onion, tomatoes, lettuce and *tostadas*. (It is a large plate!) Unlike Mexican-American cooking, where everything on the plate is heated in the oven and drenched with a *chile* sauce, each item here is separately prepared and keeps its distinctive character. The proliferation of northern style *taquerias* and steakhouses along the Border indicate that we will have increasing opportunities to enjoy this type of cooking.

The original migration of Mexicans to the United States, mostly from the north, brought about the development of what is loosely called Mexican-American cooking. Coming from the lower economic levels in Mexico, these newcomers chiefly brought recipes for the less costly dishes of their region. This is why most Mexican-

American menus are limited to *antojitos*, which represent only one, although an important element of the northern cuisine. Recently, economic problems in Mexico have led to an influx to the United States of more prosperous Mexicans. This, and the continuing popularity of such early imports as *fajitas*, is creating a growing awareness of the northern cuisine in its entirety. This trend itself is manifested in the immensely popular culinary wave of "Southwestern" cooking, much of which is based upon Mexican ingredients and mesquite broiling.

Any discussion of influences on northern Mexican cooking requires mention of New Mexico. Following the Spanish conquest, for all practical purposes New Mexico remained part of Mexico for more than two hundred years, and New Mexican cuisine evolved, as did that of the Mexican interior, from the combination of Spanish and local Indian cooking traditions. The area's major trade route, the Camino Real, ran between Chihuahua City and Santa Fe. In fact, for a short period beginning in 1824, New Mexico united with the states of Durango and Chihuahua to form the "Internal State of the North." Unlike other areas in the southwestern United States, where so-called Mexican-American food is common, the cooking of New Mexico was not brought across the Border by immigrants: the Border itself was moved south leaving the cuisine intact. The influence of the distinctive New Mexican cuisine on that of present day northern Mexico is evident in the use there of green *chiles* and green and red *chile* sauces.

An additional interesting aspect of northern Mexican cooking is its intraregional variety. Because of the region's vastness, settlements were isolated. This caused recipes to be developed more or less independently. Because of this the cuisine is much less codified than that of the more densely populated south. Names of dishes and their recipes often vary, not just from state to state, but from village to village. This is illustrated by the differences in the names of *chiles*. A *chile de árbol* in one place may be known as a *chile japonés*, or by several other names, over the next mountain. So there are sub-cuisines within the overall northern cuisine. For example, the state of Sonora produces huge, paper-thin flour *tortillas* that are not found elsewhere. In and around Monterrey, *cabrito al pastor* is very common, but less so in other areas. Except in cases where a localized dish is of particular interest, the recipes in this book have been confined to those that are common throughout the north.

El Norte: The Cooking of Northern Mexico is the product of sixteen years of research and the encouragement of many friends on both sides of the Border. The recipes were collected exclusively from Mexican cooks in restaurants, food stalls, private homes and ranches and are, as with all Mexican cooking, flexible to variation. So, for example, if a recipe is too piquant, take out the veins and seeds of the chiles to keep the flavor but lose the heat. Where appropriate, common variations are provided. The chapter on ingredients offers suitable substitutions for those which you might prefer not to use, or which might not be readily available in your area.

Unless otherwise specified, all the food recipes in this book are designed to serve four. The drinks recipes, unless otherwise noted, serve one.

Basic
Ingredients

BASIC INGREDIENTS

AVOCADOS

Guacamole, made with avocados, is served with almost every meal in northern Mexico. The two popular California avocados, the Haas and the Fuerte, are superior. The Haas, which has a rough, dark skin is preferred to the Fuerte, which has a smooth green skin. Do not use the large, smooth-skinned, Florida avocados, which either are too sweet or too watery and tasteless.

BEANS

Where beans are called for in this book, the reference is to pinto beans. As far as I can determine soaking beans will not affect their flavor, although soaking does reduce the cooking time. From my observation, Mexicans rarely soak their beans. However, it has been demonstrated that soaking beans reduces their gas-producing properties.

CHEESE

In Mexico most cheese is made by small, local operations. Even brands that are widely distributed within a region may be made in a home kitchen or garage. Northern Mexico has some of the most interesting cheeses found anywhere. From the *añejo* or *queso cotija* of Sonora to the *queso Chihuahua* or *Menenito* made by the Mennonites, they are excellent and sometimes unique.

  The cheeses most used for the recipes in this book are *asadero* and *queso Chihuahua*. *Asadero* is made by combining sour and fresh milk and consists of long braids woven together. As you might suppose, it has a slightly, but not unpleasantly, sour flavor. *Queso Chihuahua* or *queso Menenito* is made by the Mennonite community outside of Cuauhtemoc. The Mennonites are a strict religious sect from northern Europe who immigrated first to Canada and then to Mexico in the 1930s and '40s. One group acquired the 5,000 acre ranch, about two hours southwest of Chihuahua City, that used to belong to William Randolph Hearst. I pass this way nearly every year and have watched them create what is probably the most advanced and profitable farm operation in Mexico (excluding marijuana).

Unfortunately, *asadero* and *queso Menenito* are almost impossible to find in this country. Do not be fooled by domestic cheeses bearing their names. Although I have tried some that are not absolutely inedible, I do not recommend them as substitutes.

I have spent considerable time watching cheese being made in Mexico and have made it at home but I would not advise this either. For most people, the difficulty of finding unpasteurized milk, cheese presses, suitable utensils and rennet makes it impracticable. The dangers inherent in using unpasteurized milk and the fact that dry and liquid rennet react differently under different conditions compound the problem. However, for those who are interested, I have provided a general description of the process for making two types of Mexican cheese.

In dishes calling for *asadero* or *queso Menenito*, such as *chile con queso* and *queso flameado*, either mozzarella, provolone or farmer's cheese make reasonable substitutes. My favorite is an equal parts mixture of mozzarella and provolone. For dishes requiring yellow cheese, such as some of the *enchiladas* and *nachos*, use a good mild cheddar. Other substitutions will be found in the individual recipes.

Queso añejo, or *cotija*, is a flavorful cheese that crumbles easily. (When it is impregnated with chile powder it is called *queso enchilado*.) It is very difficult to melt and is used principally as a garnish for *tacos*, *enchiladas* and refried beans. A good substitute is feta cheese.

MAKING MEXICAN CHEESE

The difficulties in making cheese are not too great if you are willing to take the time to find the equipment and ingredients and to persist through a process of trial and error. But using unpasteurized milk can be dangerous. I have had no luck in trying to make cheese with supermarket milk. A few years ago many people became seriously ill, and I believe there was at least one death, from eating a domestic Mexican style cheese made of spoiled ingredients. The fact that *asadero* cheese uses day-old milk increases the risks. It would be wonderful if an American company would make authentic Mexican style cheeses for distribution, even in small quantities.

The following general guidelines, which are not exact recipes, are included for those who have a real interest and the knowledge and resources required for cheese-making. There are books dealing exclusively with this process, some of which provide sources for ingredients.

QUESO ASADERO

Nothing matches the flavor and texture of *asadero* for making *enchiladas, chile con queso* and *queso flameado*. It also is excellent for sandwiches and pizza.

Asadero is made with equal portions of fresh milk and milk that has been left at room temperature for 1 day. The amount of rennet to be added is based only on the amount of fresh milk used. This cheese is not pressed but cooked and made into strips that are then braided into balls of 1-2 pounds.

Mix the sour milk with the fresh milk, then heat to room temperature. Next add the rennet, cover with a cloth, and let the milk rest for ½-1 hour, or until coagulated.

Cut the curd as finely as possible and allow the whey to rise for about 10 minutes. Strain off the whey and add salt. Wrap the cut curds in cheese cloth and allow to drain for 3-4 hours.

Place the drained curds in a double boiler over medium heat and begin to stir. Mexican cheesemakers often use their hands and will increase the heat until it is as hot as is comfortable to the touch. The cheese is ready to be braided when you can stretch out strips an inch in diameter and 2-3 feet in length. Braid the strips into balls about the size of a small grapefruit and allow to cool.

QUESO COTIJA

This cheese is often called *queso añejo* ("aged cheese") in the south. It crumbles easily and is difficult to melt. It is used primarily as a garnish for *antojitos* and beans and is somewhat similar to a mild feta.

Heat fresh milk to room temperature and add rennet. Allow

to rest until coagulated, then cut the curds as finely as possible. Put the curds in cheesecloth and allow to drain overnight.

Remove the curds from the cheesecloth, add salt and knead into a ball for 2-3 minutes. Place the cheese in molds and press with very heavy weights for two days.

Remove the weights, brush the cheese with oil, and allow to age at room temperature for three days, wiping and re-oiling the cheese each day. Refrigerate.

CHILES

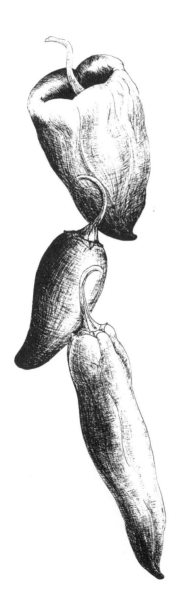

Chiles rank with *tortillas* as the most important ingredient in Mexican cooking, regardless of the region. Hardly a meal passes where *chiles*, in one form or another, are not served. One conjecture regarding the use of *chiles* in Mexican cooking holds that the traditional Indian diet of corn and beans, while reasonably nutritious, was pretty boring. The Indians, so the hypothesis goes, used *chiles* to infuse some excitement into their meals.

Chiles are currently the subject of a great deal of research as well as popular folklore, and it is often difficult to know where one ends and the other begins. We know for certain that they contain high amounts of vitamins C and A. They also may be helpful in the prevention of heart disease and stomach disorders. It is probable that ingestion of *chiles* (or rather the capsaicin which is the element which creates their heat) causes endorphins to be released in the brain. The effect is said to be similar to that of a mild dose of morphine, relieving pain and creating a general feeling of well-being. The theory is that when the body begins to feel the *chiles'* heat the brain says, "uh-oh, danger," and releases the endorphins. This may explain the fact that people who are accustomed to a regular diet of Mexican food experience serious cravings or symptoms of withdrawal when unable to partake of it for any length of time. Are we really getting high on *chiles*? Another theory, based on some research, is that consumption of *chiles* helps burn calories at an increased rate, thereby enhancing weight loss.

The neophyte will encounter a bewildering array of *chiles* from which to choose. Many cookbooks list varieties of *chile* of which the casual reader may never have heard and will never see except in Mexico or as a devoted patron of Hispanic food stores. To further frustrate the novice, most *chiles* are known by different names in their fresh and dried forns. Additional confusion is added by the tendency of different regions, and even different villages, to call the same *chile* by different names. Variations in growing conditions also produce different degrees of heat and flavor in each type. Happily for us, in northern cooking the majority of dishes utilize only a few varieties of *chile*. Even more fortunately, they are the ones that are commonly found in supermarkets in the western United States and in Hispanic groceries in other parts of the country.

"Which *chile* is hottest and by how much?," is a question that is often asked. Until recently the system commonly used for judging the heat of *chiles* was one originated by a pharmacist named Scoville early in the century. It requires five expert tasters, who sample mixtures made of different types of *chiles*, and rate the heat content of each in incremental units of 100. Three of the five must agree on the results. The measurements, expressed in "Scoville Units," range from 0 for a bell pepper to more than 250,000 for the *habanero*, the hottest pepper of all. Because of the aforementioned differences in conditions of cultivation, the same variety of *chile* may receive widely varying Scoville ratings. For example, the *chile piquín* ranges from 44,000 units to more than 70,000 units. As you can see, the system is less than exact and the results can be confusing. To remedy this the staff of *The Whole Chile Pepper* magazine (Albuquerque, New Mexico), an excellent publication for aficionados of *picante* foods, has developed a simplified heat index scale. The scale, based upon the Scoville system, rates *chiles* from 1 to 10, with 1 being mildest and 10 hottest. The ratings are verified by high pressure liquefied chromatography (HPLC) testing, which measures capsaicin in *chiles* in parts per million. These heat scale ratings will be provided in the following descriptions of individual *chiles*.

Chiles, as mentioned earlier, come in two forms: fresh and dried.

FRESH CHILES

Fresh *chiles* are used in the preparation of sauces and to flavor beef, chicken, pork and fish dishes. In *salsas crudas* (uncooked sauces), the *chiles* are chopped or diced and mixed with the other ingredients, such as onions and tomatoes. Fresh *chiles* are often broiled first for cooked sauces, complementing the wonderful smoky flavor typical of so many northern dishes.

To broil fresh *chiles*, place them on a grill over a wood or charcoal fire and cook, turning them often until the skins are well charred. This also can be done in an oven broiler by placing the *chiles* on a metal cookie sheet about 6 to 8 inches from the heating element and proceeding as above.

Some dishes, such as *chile rellenos*, call for *chiles* to be skinned. Many cookbooks suggest that skinning is facilitated by broiling or roasting the *chiles* over a gas flame, then placing them in a polyethelene bag to "sweat" for 20 minutes before peeling. I find that a better method is to fry them in deep oil at 350-375 degrees for 30 to 40 seconds, or until the skins have turned completely white (as they separate from the *chile*). I then place them in a plastic bag for about 10 minutes, after which they can be easily peeled. This method also preserves the firmness of the *chiles*.

CHILE JALAPENO

The *jalapeño* is probably the most familiar *chile* to most Americans and is slightly less piquant than the *serrano*, at 5 on the heat scale. It is sold fresh and pickled in most parts of this country. Never use the pickled *jalapeño* as a substitute for the fresh version. A serrano may be used instead.

CHILE POBLANO

The *chile poblano* is named for the area around *Puebla* and is one of the oldest *chiles* indigenous to Mexico. It is also called *chile para rellenar*, or *chile* for stuffing, as it is used to make *chile rellenos*. The *chile poblano* is large, often 5 inches long and 3 inches in diameter, and has an attractive dark green color. The *poblano* has a heat scale rating of 3 to 4. The *chile anaheim*, or green *chile*, is a good substitute.

CHILE SERRANO

Although the *jalapeño* is much better known, the *serrano* is the favorite *chile* throughout the north. It is about 1½-2½ inches long and ¼-⅓ inch in diameter. Ranging between 6 and 7 on the heat scale, this is one of the hottest of the fresh *chiles* used in our recipes. As is true in all cases, using a different *chile* will produce a different but equally tasty result. In this case, *jalapeños* are the best substitute.

CHILE VERDE, CALIFORNIO OR ANAHEIM

This *chile* is usually called *chile verde* or green *chile.* It was originally developed in New Mexico and California and is as long as the *poblano* but narrower. It is usually the mildest of the fresh *chiles*, being rated at 2 on the heat scale, but it is sometimes hotter. This *chile*, like the *jalapeño* and *serrano*, is widely available in western American supermarkets in both fresh and canned forms. Use it fresh whenever possible. The *chile poblano* may be substituted for the *anaheim*.

DRIED CHILES

Dried *chiles* are usually used to make sauces. Many recipes call for the *chiles* to be toasted and / or softened.

To toast dried *chiles*, first warm a *comal* or heavy iron skillet over low heat before cooking the *chiles*. Turn them constantly until they are softened and fragrant. Take care to avoid burning.

To soften dried chiles, place them in a bowl and cover them with very hot or boiling water and let them sit for at least 10 minutes. If they are very dry, 20 to 30 minutes will be required.

To seed dry *chiles*, slit them down one side with a sharp pointed knife and remove the seeds, stem and as many of the veins as possible.

CHILE ANCHO

The *chile ancho* is the dried *chile poblano.* This *chile*, rates 3 to 4 on the heat scale. It is usually about 3-4½ inches long and 2-3 inches wide. If this *chile* is not obtainable, substitute either a dried New Mexico or Anaheim *chile*, or use 1 tablespoon of mild *chile* powder for each *chile* called for in the recipe. However, since *chile* powder often contains ground cumin, oregano and salt and, in most cases, the seeds too, the result will be a slightly more bitter and less rounded taste.

CHILE DE ARBOL
The *chile de árbol* is longer, thinner and has a smoother texture than the wrinkled *chile japonés*. Because of its long, thin shape, it is often called *pico de pájaro* (bird's beak). The *chile de árbol* rates a 7 on the heat scale. Substitute ¼ teaspoon of cayenne for each *chile de árbol*.

CHILE CHIPOTLE
The *chile chipotle* is the *jalapeño* which has been dried and smoked. It is available in dried form, or canned with *adobo* sauce. For a short-cut *adobo* sauce, mix 6 pickled *jalapeños* with ⅓ cup tomato sauce and 1 teaspoon of liquid smoke.

CHILE JAPONES
The *chile japonés* is often described as a dried *chile serrano*. In fact, it both looks and tastes like a dried *serrano*. However, experts contend it is not the dried *serrano*, but a small cayenne variety, although some believe it to be a *piquín* variety. It takes its name from the fact that it is widely grown in Japan and other parts of the Orient. It is very hot and is used extensively in oriental recipes and Indian curries and is therefore widely available in oriental as well as Hispanic food stores. For the recipes in this book that call for *japonés* or *chile de árbol*, use the *árbol*, if available. It has a smoother texture and flavor. The *japonés* is mentioned principally because it is a good substitute and easy to find. Although not officially rated, the *chile japonés* probably rates a 6-7 on the heat scale. As a substitute, use ¼ teaspoon cayenne pepper for each *japonés*.

CHILE PASILLA
The *chile pasilla* is very similar to the *ancho* except that it is thinner, longer and darker in color. In fact, *anchos* are often called

chiles pasillas, especially in Baja California. However, the *pasilla* has the same heat rating as the *ancho*.

CHILE PIQUIN AND CHILE TEPIN

Chile piquín and *tepín* are essentially the same. Although about the same size, they have different shapes. They grow wild in many parts of northern Mexico, where villagers gather them by the basketful to be dried or pickled for future use. In fact, they are so abundant in the wild and so easy to grow at home that, compared with other varieties, very little is planted commercially. The *piquín* is the hottest *chile* used in the recipes that follow, and, as with all *chiles*, extreme caution must be exercised in handling them. The *piquín* and *tepín* are rated at a formidable 8 to 9 on the heat scale. The *chile piquín* is very small, usually less than ¼ inch long, and shaped like a tiny football. The *tepín*, often called *chiltepín* (its original name in the Nahuatl language), is about the same size but round. Because of their size, these *chiles* are not seeded before use. They make ornamental, as well as useful, pot plants.

CILANTRO

The English word for this parsley-like plant is coriander. In the Southwest, where it is found in most supermarkets, it is almost always called by its Spanish name. It has a particular affinity for *chiles* and is used in many northern Mexican sauces. *Cilantro* is an ingredient in many ethnic cuisines, including East Indian, African, Southeast Asian and Chinese. In fact, it is often called Chinese parsley. However, do not let this terminology mislead you: parsley is no substitute for *cilantro*, nor is there one. While parsley provides a subtle flavor and a garnish effect, coriander has a distinctive flavor for which there is no substitute. Ground coriander, which is made from the seeds and is often used in southern Mexico and other parts of the world, is also no substitute for fresh. *Cilantro* is easily grown in the greenhouse or garden. It does well in cool to moderate temperatures and grows very quickly.

COOKING OIL

Unless you must, do not economize on cooking oil. In deep frying, a cheap oil will break down much sooner than a good one. There is nothing worse for cooking than an inferior olive oil. Use extra virgin olive oil whenever possible; or select a good peanut, soy or safflower oil.

CORN HUSKS

Corn husks are used for wrapping *tamales* and can be purchased in supermarkets in the Southwest and in Latin American groceries elsewhere. You can also dry your own husks or, in a pinch, use a thin parchment paper or white cloth, such as an old pillow slip.

CREAM

In northern Mexico, cream is often used as a topping for *enchiladas* and *tacos*. Their cream is thick and fresh, resembling the *crème fraiche* of France. Sour cream can be substituted, but it is much better to make your own cream. Mix 1 tablespoon of buttermilk with 1 cup whipping cream, let the mixture stand at room temperature for 5-6 hours, then refrigerate.

CUMIN

Cumin, *comino* in Spanish, is an herb used in many northern recipes, usually in combination with oregano. Use only the whole cumin, as the ground is much blander.

GARLIC OIL

Garlic oil is used for basting meats before, during and after broiling; in the dressing for Caesar Salad; and for other dishes when a touch of garlic is desired.

Peel 10 cloves of garlic and bruise them slightly by pressing with the flat edge of a cook's knife or cleaver. Place the cloves in a medium-sized bottle or jar (a salad dressing cruet is perfect) and add 1 cup of a good cooking or olive oil. Refrigerate the container or the oil will lose its freshness. When you have used about ⅔ of the oil, refill the container with oil, as the same cloves can be used until they begin to lose their pungency. When the preserved cloves are removed they can be chopped and substituted for fresh garlic.

LARD

Our commercial lards are much blander than those used in Mexico. To render your own lard, place 2 cups of chopped pork fat in a heatproof sauce pan in a 300 degree oven and cook for about 1 hour, turning every 10 minutes.

In parts of the north, beef suet is used instead of lard. The flavor is excellent and is particularly interesting when used to make flour *tortillas*. Render the beef suet or fat according to the above directions for rendering lard.

With today's emphasis on diet and health, people prefer not to use saturated fats such as lard. The same quantity of vegetable shortening (as indicated for lard) can be substituted when making flour *tortillas*, *empanadas* and *tamales*, and good cooking oil when making other items.

LIMES

When a Mexican uses the Spanish word *limón*, he is referring to a lime. Lemons are virtually nonexistent in Mexico and there is no word in Spanish which distinguishes the two. Mexican limes are small and very tart. The large, seedless Persian limes may be substituted, but they are sweeter. Lemons can, of course, be used, but the taste imparted will be altogether different. In any case, never use frozen or reconstituted lemon or lime juice.

OREGANO

Oregano also should be used whole rather than ground. This flavorful herb should be used in moderation as it has a very strong flavor. It is closely related to marjoram and in many places is known as wild marjoram.

PUMPKIN SEEDS

For recipes which include pumpkin seeds, do not use the commercially roasted seeds. Buy them raw from a health food store and roast them yourself.

SESAME SEEDS

Sesame seeds are usually toasted for Mexican recipes. To toast the seeds, place them in an ungreased skillet over low heat and stir constantly until they are nicely browned. Care should be taken, as they burn easily.

SOUR ORANGE JUICE

Although orange juice is not as much used in cooking in the north of Mexico as in the south, it is an ingredient in the recipes for *carnitas de jugo*, *puerco en adobo* and *pollo en pipián*. Mexicans usually use the juice of the sour or Seville orange for cooking. If you are unable to obtain sour oranges, add 2 tablespoons of lime juice to 6 ounces of fresh orange juice for a substitute. (Never use frozen concentrated juice as it is too syrupy.)

TOMATILLOS

Tomatillos, often called *tomates verdes*, look like small green tomatoes. However, they are actually a relative of the gooseberry. *Tomatillos*, which turn slightly yellow when ripe, are almost always used in their unripe stage, when they are a lovely, bright green color. They are now often sold fresh in the southwestern United States and can be found canned for use in sauces, or in prepared sauces, in other parts of the country. The widely distributed La Victoria and Herdez brands offer good *tomatillo* sauces, although the Herdez is too salty for my taste. However, canned or bottled *tomatillos* in any form are a poor substitute for fresh. *Tomatillos* are easily grown at home and make an attractive plant. Because they are used in their unripe form, *tomatillos* must be simmered for 10 to 15 minutes before being incorporated into recipes. Put them in cold water and bring them slowly to the boil to prevent the skins from splitting.

VINEGAR

Northern Mexicans regularly use four types of vinegar: wine, white, apple, rice, and cane. Cane is the favorite for most uses, particularly in making sauces. As our commercial vinegars are much stronger than the Mexican, they should be diluted with 1 part water to 1 part vinegar.

1. Quick and tasty snacks are available from street vendors all over northern Mexico. A taco vendor in Chichuaha City prepares for the mid-morning rush.

2. In northern Mexico, much of the shopping is done in *fruterias*, small grocery stores, specializing in fruits and vegetables.

3. The use of oxen to haul fire wood and perform other chores illustrates the timlessness and simplicity of life in many parts of northern Mexico.

4. *Bistec Pimental*, sizzling T-bone steaks smothered with vine-ripened, mild chiles is a favorite in Chihuahua's steakhouses as well as at picnics as pictured on the right.

6. The blended fragrances of mesquite and wild flowers typify the popular *Carne asada*, northern style picnics, which evolved from the area's ranching heritage.

5. An outdoor produce display tempts passersby at a typical grocery.

7. *Carnitas*, a specialty of the State of Michoacan, is also enjoyed throughout the North.

8. A courtyard entry in the 17th century village of Bustamante, famous for its "dulces" or sweets.

10. Many Tarahumara Indians of Chichuahua still live in either caves or cabin-like homes, dwellings well suited to their mountain environment.

11. Salsas, which come in a variety of flavors, textures and piquancy are an integral part of every northern meal.

9. Northern Mexico is famous for its indoor-outdoor steakhouses, such as this one in Sabinas Hidalgo in the State of Nuevo León.

12. Although supermarkets have found their way to Mexico, open-air produce markets are still an important part of community life.

13. An Indian girl prepares *gorditas*, high in Chihua-hua's Barrancas del Cobre or Copper Canyon.

14. In Baja California, eating establishments of all types share the incomparable backdrop and views of the Pacific Ocean.

KITCHEN
EQUIPMENT

EQUIPMENT

BEAN MASHER

This device consists of a circle of steel with holes drilled in it, about ¼ inch thick and about 4 inches in diameter. A handle is attached to the center. It is used to mash cooked beans in the preparation of refried beans. A heavy slotted cooking spoon also may be used for this purpose.

BLENDER

Blenders or *licuadoras* are becoming very popular in northern Mexico. They can be great labor savers, but their limitations must be well understood. They are most useful for making sauces from dried *chiles*, grinding the ingredients quickly and producing excellent smooth-textured sauces. They should, however, never be used for making sauces from fresh *chiles* and tomatoes. The result is normally a frothy mess. Fresh sauces should always be made with a *molcajete*.

COMAL

A *comal* is a long iron Mexican griddle that is made to fit over two stove burners. It is used primarily in the north for making and warming *tortillas*. A heavy iron skillet is an excellent substitute.

COOKWARE

For Mexican cooking, considering cost and quality, nothing beats good old iron skillets and dutch ovens. They are durable and heavy enough to be used over an open fire and perfectly maintain an evenness of heating. Equip yourself with small, medium and large iron skillets, as well as a medium-sized dutch oven.

FOOD PROCESSOR

For many types of cooking, a food processor, if properly used, can be a servant in the kitchen. I find it most useful for grating cheese, making *tortilla* dough and grinding meat. It is also good for chopping large quantities of vegetables, although I think chopping by hand produces a better, more uniform result. As an alternative to making a fresh *chile*–tomato sauce from scratch, a food processor will do a much better job than a blender.

LIME JUICER

When making drinks that contain lime juice, Mexicans always squeeze the juice fresh. They have a juicer that, while simple, is the most efficient I have ever seen for squeezing small quantities (see illustration). They are available in cookware shops and Hispanic food stores.

MOLCAJETE

This is perhaps the most useful piece of equipment in the Mexican kitchen. A *molcajete* is a mortar and pestle, Mexican style. Made of black basalt, the rough surface is ideal for grinding spices and is almost the only utensil that will allow you to mash *chiles*, onions, tomatoes and other ingredients into a sauce of the proper consistency. The most practical size of *molcajete* for home use is approximately 8 inches in diameter. In Mexican homes, table sauces are often served in the *molcajete* in which they were made, providing an efficient and attractive presentation. While they are difficult to find in some parts of the country, a search of Hispanic food stores will usually be rewarded. The Japanese rough mortar and pestle is a good substitute, but if neither is available an ordinary smooth mortar and pestle will do.

POTTERY

Nothing tastes better than beans and stews cooked in Mexican pottery and nothing looks better than *antojitos* served on hand-painted Mexican plates. However, I have a beautiful collection of Mexican pottery that I almost never use, because Mexican artisans still use lead-based finishes on pottery and health officials contend this can be very dangerous. So I use American-made pottery instead, which is not as authentic but safer. When preparing oven-baked dishes like *enchiladas*, be sure to use well-fired pottery to avoid breakage. I have found Francoma ware from Oklahoma to be both well-made and attractive.

TORTILLA PRESS

A *tortilla* press is a must if you live in an area where freshly made corn *tortillas* are not readily available. Even if they are, you will find that, as with many other foods, the home-made variety have both better flavor and texture. *Tortilla* presses can be purchased or ordered at specialty food and cookware stores.

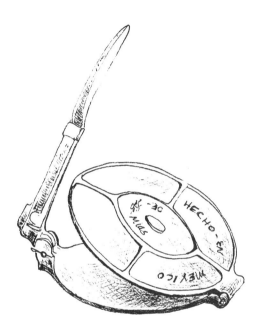

RECIPES

Drinks

BEBIDAS

There is a saying in northern Mexico, "*No hay sabados sin sol y domingos sin borrachos*": There are no Saturdays without sun nor Sundays without drunks. In spite of a popular misconception, Mexicans are very hard-working and particularly so in the north where they are as tough and rugged as the land itself. However, they also believe that there must be a time set aside to relax and to blow off steam. Saturday is often chosen for this purpose. The results are often all too plain on Sunday, as partygoers return home for the traditional day of winding down with the family before the work week begins.

In their choice of drinks, the average northerner is somewhat more sophisticated than his counterpart in the south. It is not uncommon to see such exotic drinks as Planter's Punch and Singapore Slings on the menus of northern restaurants. This is mostly due to the fact that during Prohibition *gringos* came by the thousands to the free and easy Mexican border towns. Places like Tijuana, Ciudad Juárez and Nuevo Laredo built elegant establishments, and fortunes, catering to North American taste, and the influence remains.

Although drinks of all types are consumed in Mexico, I have found the following to be, by far, the most popular in northern Mexico.

Unless otherwise noted, each of these recipes makes one drink serving.

TEQUILA SOUR

1 shot tequila
1 shot lime juice
1 shot simple syrup (see index)

This drink is far more popular among Mexicans than the Margarita.

Pour ingredients over ice in a bar mixer, cover, and shake for 20 to 30 seconds, strain into a sour glass or serve on the rocks. Garnish with an orange slice and cherry.

TEQUILA SUNRISE

Fill a 12 ounce tumbler with ice and add 1 shot of tequila. Fill the glass with freshly squeezed orange juice and top with a dash or two of grenadine. Serve with a straw or stir the drink to blend the grenadine.

DON CHUY

1 shot vodka
1 shot lime juice
clamato juice
Worcestershire sauce
tabasco sauce
club soda

I have named this drink for the colorful character who first made it for me at a carne asada (cookout) on the Sabinas river in northern Coahuila. It is an excellent alternative to a Bloody Mary.

Pour the vodka over ice into a 12 ounce tumbler. Add the lime juice, then fill with clamato juice. Add about three dashes of both Worcestershire and tabasco, top with soda, then stir.

TOM COLLINS

1 shot gin
1 shot simple syrup (see index)
1 shot lime juice
club soda

Fill a tall bar glass with ice, gin, syrup and lime juice. Add club soda and stir.

1-2-3

1 shot tequila
½ small lime
salt

This is probably the most popular way to drink tequila in Mexico. Use the best tequila available or suffer the consequences.

Place a small amount of salt on the soft fleshy part of your left hand (if you are right-handed) between the thumb and forefinger. Lick the salt and drink the shot of *tequila* (which is held in your other hand). Finally, bite into the lime half. Then hold on!

There is some dispute over the best order in which to take the tequila, salt and lime. Experiment and adopt your favorite. There are six different combinations, so don't try them all at one sitting!

BEER

Mexican beers, like European beers, and indeed like beers in almost all parts of the world except the United States, are distinctive, each one brewed to have its own special character. Most Mexican beer is brewed in the industrial city of Monterrey, which is also the home of *cabrito al pastor* (they make a wonderful combination). However, some excellent beers are brewed in other parts of the country, including Chihuahua and Yucatán. Many Mexican beers are now exported, so you can try them all to determine your favorite. You might begin with the following: Bohemia, Corona, Tecate, Dos Equis, Carta Blanca, Chihuahua, and Negra Modelo.

SIMPLE SYRUP

1 cup water
½ cup sugar

Mix the sugar and water; then heat, stirring the liquid until it just begins to simmer. Cool and store in a glass or heavy plastic container. A pancake syrup dispenser is a good choice. Refrigerate if the syrup will not be used within a day or two.

COCA-COLA

Coca-Cola is the traditional *refresco* of northern Mexico. One sees Cokes everywhere. In fact, in Mexican homes in which I have taken meals, a liter of Coke was placed on the dining room table, much as we would a pitcher of water. It is interesting to note that Mexican Coke is noticeably sweeter than that in the United States and many *aficionados* who live close to the Border regularly bring it back by the case.

LEMONADE

For a good portion of the year, northern Mexico is very hot and dry and nothing is more refreshing than an ice-cold lemonade. "Lemonade" is actually a misnomer for the drink sold by street vendors from 5-8 gallon jugs, since it is always made with lime juice. Mexicans almost always sweeten it with a sugar syrup, instead of the plain sugar we use, which gives their drink a distinctive flavor.

For one glass of lemonade, place 3 tablespoons lime juice in a 12 ounce glass filled with ice. Add 2 to 3 tablespoons simple syrup, or sweeten to taste. Fill the glass with water and stir.

To make one quart of lemonade, mix ⅔ cup lime juice, ⅔ cup simple syrup and 2⅔ cups water in a pitcher. Place in the refrigerator to cool.

MARGARITA

1 shot tequila
1 shot lime juice
1 shot triple sec
salt

The Margarita is the favorite drink of Americans when they go to Mexican-American restaurants. When traveling in Mexico, they are surprised to discover that it is difficult to find a bartender who can make this drink, except in tourist oriented establish-

ments. The reason is that Mexicans rarely drink Margaritas.

Rub the rim of a martini glass or specially designed Margarita glass with a half lime, then dip the dampened rim into salt to coat it.

Pour the tequila, lime juice and triple sec over ice in a bar mixer, cover and shake for 20 to 30 seconds. Strain the mixture into the salted glass or serve on the rocks; or blend with the ice to make a frozen Margarita. Garnish with a lime wedge.

RAMOS GIN FIZZ

1 Tbs. powdered sugar
juice of 1 lemon or lime
white of 1 egg
10 drops orange flavor water
1 oz. gin
2 oz. milk

This is the original recipe from the famous Cadillac Bar in Nuevo Laredo.

Shake all ingredients over ice in a cocktail shaker for 30 seconds. Strain and serve.

SANGRÍA

2 cups port wine
⅔ cup fresh orange juice
juice of 1 lime
3 oz. brandy
1 orange, sliced

There are many versions of this wine punch, which originated in Spain. This recipe was given to me by a friend in Monterrey.

Mix all ingredients in a pitcher and chill for several hours. Serve in tall glasses over ice. Fill the glasses about ¾ full, add club soda and stir briefly. Serves two.

RUM AND COKE

1 shot dark rum
Coca-Cola
¼ lime wedge (optional)

In addition to being a major producer of rum, Mexico is also a major consumer of this product. Rum mixed with Coca-Cola is the favorite rum drink in all of Mexico. It is called Cuba Libre when ¼ lime, squeezed, is added.

Pour the rum over ice cubes into an 8 ounce bar glass, fill with Coke and stir briefly. Squeeze the lime and add to the glass, if desired.

RUM COLLINS

This drink is the same as a Tom Collins, except that it is made with light rum rather than gin.

BRANDY

In addition to tequila and rum, Mexico produces a large amount of brandy. The local brandies, while not equal to their European counterparts, are acceptable and economical alternatives. Brandy is often drunk straight, after dinner, but it is also popular at parties. At a *carne asada* (picnic or barbecue), people typically will begin by drinking beer, then switch to brandy, usually mixed with Coca-Cola or club soda, or a mixture of both. The most popular brandy is Presidente, which is available in this country.

SANGRÍTA

2 cups fresh squeezed orange juice
3 Tbs. grenadine
¼ heaping tsp. cayenne pepper (or to taste)
2 tsp. salt

Sangríta is most often used as a chaser with tequila, or mixed with it to make a vampiro. In Mexico, Sangríta is sold in bottles, but this fresh, home-made version is far better.

Stir all ingredients together until thoroughly combined.

VAMPIRO

1½ oz. tequila
sangrita (see following recipe)
club soda (optional)
lime wedge

This drink is very popular in the States of Coahuila and Nuevo León.

Pour tequila into a tall glass over ice cubes and add sangrita. Add soda, if preferred. Garnish with a lime wedge.

HORCHATA

1 ripe cantaloupe, 1¾-2 lbs.
¼ cup lime juice
2 Tbs. sugar
½ tsp. vanilla

Horchata is an extremely refreshing soft drink, popular throughout Mexico. It is variously made with dried melon seeds, rice, nuts and fruit, often in different combinations. This simplified northern version is my favorite and a wonderful antidote to the area's dry, hot summers. It makes a great fruit punch, to which you may add a little gin or rum. This is a good example of the type of recipe that can be modified to suit your taste. Use more or less sugar, lime juice and vanilla, or add some almonds or cooked rice to the mixture before blending.

Cut the cantaloupe in half and scoop out as much as possible of the flesh and seeds. There should be about 2-2½ cups. Place in the jar of a blender. Add the other ingredients and 2-3 cups water and blend for 2 minutes. Strain and refrigerate or serve over ice.

Sauces
SALSAS

Salsas, tortillas and beans are the mainstays of Mexican cooking. A bowl of some kind of hot sauce, or perhaps several, is always on the dining table. In years of traveling in Mexico, I have encountered the many excellent variations included here. The secret of a successful sauce is always to use fresh ingredients.

Warning: exercise extreme care when handling chiles. They can cause severe burns. The use of rubber gloves is recommended. Wash your hands thoroughly and never touch your eyes or other sensitive areas after handling chiles.

Almost all of the following sauces may be eaten with *tostadas* as a snack or appetizer. It might be fun to make one bowl of each and have a tasting party to become familiar with them and select your favorites. However, be sure to warn your friends about some of the hotter selections, such as *salsa de chile piquín.*

Sauce recipes serve four.

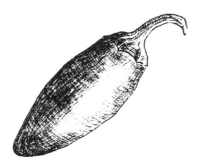

Salsa de Jalapeño en Escabeche

Pickled Jalapeño Sauce

3 medium tomatoes, broiled and
finely chopped
2-3 pickled jalapeños, minced
1½ Tbs. juice from jalapeño can
or jar
¾ tsp. oregano
¼ tsp. salt
⅓ cup onion, minced
1½ tsp. olive oil
1-2 cloves garlic, minced

This excellent table sauce from Durango is especially good with tostadas. The pickled jalapeños, even though canned, add a unique flavor that works well with the other ingredients.

Place the oil and garlic in a small saucepan over very low heat. Cook until the garlic is soft but not browned, 1-2 minutes. Add the remaining ingredients, stirring to mix well. Bring the sauce to a boil over medium heat, and, turning the heat to low, simmer for 5 minutes. Allow to cool before serving.

Salsa Jalapeño Cocido

Cooked Jalapeño Sauce

2 medium tomatoes, peeled and
chopped
2 or 3 medium jalapeños,
minced
⅓ medium onion, finely
chopped
1 medium garlic clove, minced
1 Tbs. cooking oil
2 tsp. vinegar
½ tsp. salt, or to taste
¼ cup loosely packed, chopped
cilantro

This sauce, popular in the northern states of Coahuila and Tamaulipas, is a favorite in Texas restaurants. But the Texas version, usually made with canned ingredients, is inferior to the original.

Heat the oil over medium heat and saute the *jalapeños*, onion and garlic until soft but not browned.

Add the tomatoes, vinegar and salt and simmer uncovered for 5 minutes or until the desired consistency is reached. Remove the pan from the heat and add the chopped *cilantro*.

Cool and serve with tostadas or other foods of your choice.

SALSA DE JALAPEÑO
O SERRANO ASADO

Broiled Jalapeño or Serrano Sauce

**2 medium to large tomatoes,
    broiled**

**1-2 chiles jalapeños, or 2-3
    chiles serranos, broiled**

¼ tsp. salt, or to taste

*This simple salsa is one of the best all-purpose table sauces in
either of its forms: ground; or blended and strained. The charred
tomatoes and chiles add a robust flavor, and the texture is yours
to determine. Because of the differences between jalapeños and
serranos in size and amount of heat, it is difficult to specify the
exact number of chiles to be used. A little experimentation will
quickly provide the right formula for your taste.*

As mentioned above, there are two ways to make this sauce, each
producing quite different results. The easiest method, and perhaps my favorite, is to put all the ingredients into a blender and
blend for about 30 seconds, then strain into a serving bowl. The
texture will be smooth and the sauce flecked with tiny bits of the
charred tomato and *chile* skins. The other method requires that
the chile seeds be removed, then all ingredients ground to the
desired consistency in a *molcajete* or mortar and pestle. (Alter-
nately, a few whirls in a food processor will work, but it is easy to
overprocess.) The result makes a chunky, textured sauce with lots
of color.

NOTE: To broil tomatoes and *chiles*, place 3-6 inches above hot
coals on a grill, or below the oven's broiler. Broil until they are
soft and the skins are well charred, 10-15 minutes.

Salsa de Chile Piquín

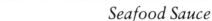

Chile Piquín Sauce

¼ cup chile piquín

2 Tbs. mild cider vinegar

¼ cup diced onion

⅓ cup water

1 medium clove garlic

¼ tsp. salt, or to taste

1 small or ½ medium tomato

Beware! This sauce is made with the fiery little chile piquín and these tiny, football-shaped chiles pack quite a wallop. The sauce adds piquance to mesquite-broiled meats, but be sure to use sparingly. This recipe comes from San Luís de Río Colorado, a large city thirty miles south of Yuma, Arizona. One fine restaurant there serves nothing but lamb tacos accompanied by this sauce.

Place all ingredients in the jar of a blender and blend for one minute. Use only a few drops (until you get the "feel" of it) on broiled meats, especially lamb.

Salsa Para Mariscos

Seafood Sauce

2 Tbs. lime juice

¼ cup olive oil or other good
    quality cooking oil

2 large chiles poblanos or
    anaheim, minced

3 chiles serranos, minced

1 clove garlic, minced

1 tsp. oregano

pinch salt, or to taste

pinch pepper, or to taste

2 Tbs. chopped, loosely packed
    cilantro

This sauce is delicious with cold, boiled shrimp and is an excellent alternative to the usual thick, red seafood sauces.

Mix all ingredients well and allow to stand at room temperature for 1 hour before serving.

SALSA DE TOMATILLO

Tomatillo Sauce

½ lb. tomatillos
¼ tsp. sugar
1 chile serrano, seeded
¼ tsp. salt
⅓ cup water

This sauce is served with tacos, broiled seafood and chicken and as an enchilada sauce. It is best made with fresh tomatillos, but canned may be substituted. The following recipe is for use as a table sauce. For use as an enchilada sauce, double the quantities to serve four.

If using fresh *tomatillos*, bring slowly to a boil in a small sauce pan in order to prevent the skins from breaking. Simmer gently for about 10 minutes or until they are very tender. If using the cooked, canned *tomatillos*, be sure to rinse them thoroughly.

Place the *tomatillos* in a blender or food processor with the remaining ingredients and blend or process until puréed. Return the sauce to the pan and simmer for 5 minutes or until the sauce has thickened slightly.

SALSA DE CHILE ÁRBOL

Chile Arbol Sauce

1 oz. chiles de árbol or chiles japonéses
2 Tbs. cane or cider vinegar
½ cup water
2 cloves garlic
¼ tsp. cumin
½ tsp. oregano
½ tsp. salt

This is one of the hottest sauces I have ever tried. It takes a confirmed "chile head" to enjoy it!

Toast the *chiles* by heating them in a heavy skillet over low heat until they are fragrant but not burned.

Place the *chiles* in a blender with ¼ cup of the water and the remaining ingredients and blend for 1 minute. Add the remaining water and blend again for 30 seconds. Strain the sauce into a bowl.

SALSA BORRACHA

Drunken Sauce

1 small chile pasilla or ancho

2 dried chiles chipotles

1 chile de árbol

2 medium tomatoes, broiled

½ medium onion, diced

½ Tbs. cooking oil

¼ tsp. salt

½ Tbs. mescal or tequila, or to
taste

This sauce is especially suited to charbroiled meats because it uses the smoked chile chipotle.

Toast the *chiles* by placing in a heavy skillet over low heat. Turn frequently, until they just begin to color and give off a pungent fragrance. Avoid burning, as this will make them bitter. After toasting, soak the *chiles* in hot water for ½ hour. Next, seed them and place them in the jar of a blender.

Broil the tomatoes, place one of them in the blender with the *chiles*, and blend for 1 minute. In a small saucepan, saute the onion in the oil over low heat for 5 minutes. Then add the blended *chile* mixture, the salt and *mescal* or *tequila*, and cook another 5 minutes. Crush the remaining tomato in a *molcajete* or mortar and pestle and mix with the other ingredients in a serving bowl. The second tomato may also be whirled 2-3 times in a food processor. However, be sure to turn off the processor before it loses its texture.

SALSA DE CHILE VERDE

Green Chile Sauce

3 medium tomatoes

4 green chiles, broiled

⅓ medium onion, diced

1 tsp. vinegar

¼ tsp. salt, or to taste

¼ cup loosely packed cilantro,
chopped

This sauce is a specialty of the state of Sonora.

Broil and then dice the tomatoes. Broil the *chiles*, place them in a polyethelene bag for 15 to 20 minutes, then peel, seed and dice them.

Mix the tomatoes and *chiles* with the remaining ingredients.

SALSA DE CHILE ANCHO

Ancho Chile Sauce

3 chiles anchos, stemmed,
    seeded and deveined
2 cloves garlic
½ tsp. salt, or to taste
water

This is a fairly mild but robust sauce that is particularly good with pork or tostadas.

Soak the *chiles* in hot water for at least 15 minutes, then place in a blender with the garlic, salt, and ½ cup of the water in which the *chiles* were soaked. Blend at high speed for 1 minute, adding water and continuing to blend until the desired consistency is achieved.

    As a variation, add a broiled tomato to the sauce.

SALSA DE JALAPEÑO VERDE

Green Jalapeño Sauce

3 oz. fresh jalapeños, stems
    removed
1 tsp. white vinegar
¼ cup water
1 tsp. salt
¼ tsp. sugar

This sauce, made of puréed jalapeños, is very hot. It is delicious if used sparingly over broiled meats and poultry.

Place the *chiles* in a saucepan and cover with water. Bring to a boil and simmer until they are soft, about 15 minutes. Slice open the *chiles* and remove all the seeds with a small spoon. Next, put the cooked *chiles* in a blender with the ¼ cup of water and the remaining ingredients and blend until puréed, about 30 seconds. Allow to cool before serving.

SALSA CRUDA DE CHIHUAHUA

Uncooked Sauce from Chihuahua

¼ cup chile serrano, seeded and chopped

¼ cup chile jalapeño, seeded and chopped

¼ cup chile poblano or verde, seeded and chopped

¼ cup onion, chopped

2 Tbs. green onion, chopped

¼-½ tsp. salt, or to taste

½ cup fresh squeezed lime juice

2 medium tomatoes, chopped

1 medium tomato, broiled and blended until smooth

¼ cup cilantro, minced

1 medium avocado, peeled, seeded and chopped (optional)

This sauce may be misnamed, as the lime juice "cooks" the chiles, softening the bite, as it does with ceviche.

Place the *chiles*, onion, green onion and salt in a glass or other nonreactive bowl with the lime juice. Mix well and refrigerate for 1-2 hours. Strain off and discard the lime juice. Next, add the chopped tomatoes and just enough of the broiled, blended tomato to bind the mixture into a sauce. Add more salt, if desired. Stir in the *cilantro* and avocado, if used. The avocado, although optional, adds a great deal to the sauce.

NOTE: To broil the tomato, place 3-6 inches above hot coals on a grill or below the oven's broiler. Broil until the tomato is soft and the skin is well charred, 10-15 minutes.

PICO DE GALLO

Tomato & Chile Relish

1 medium tomato, seeded and finely chopped

3 chiles serranos, seeded and minced

2 medium green onions, minced

3 Tbs. onion, finely chopped

⅛ tsp. salt, or to taste

¼ cup lightly packed, chopped cilantro

1 tsp. lime juice (optional)

Literally translated, pico de gallo means "rooster's beak." No one has been able to explain to me the significance of this name. Perhaps it derives from the shape of the serrano peppers. In the north of Mexico, pico de gallo is the universal table relish. It always accompanies fajitas (skirt steak), whether served as an entree or chopped in tacos. It is delicious with any broiled meat and is an attractive garnish on most Mexican plates.

Toss all ingredients until well mixed and serve immediately, as this relish does not keep.

Appetizers

APERITIVOS Y BOTANAS

Most cookbooks fail to make clear the real distinction between *aperitivos* and *botanas*, on the one hand, and *antojitos*, on the other. Usually, all three are inaccurately classified as appetizers.

We think of an appetizer as a small first course, served before the entree, to stimulate the palate. The Spanish word *aperitivo*, "that which has the power of opening the appetite," closely fits this concept. The *Botana*, literally the "plug or stopple used to stop up the opening in a leather wine bag," in Mexico refers to snacks taken with cocktails, such as peanuts and *pepitas*. However, both *aperitivos* and *botanas* may be considered to be appetizers, as we know them.

Antojito is a form of the Spanish word *antojo*: a whim, vehement desire, longing, hankering, or fancy. So, *antojitos* could be literally translated as little whims or fancies, or, as they are often used in Mexico, snacks. However, *antojitos*, as in *"antojitos Mexicanos"* also refers to typical Mexican dishes. Many Mexican restaurants advertise *antojitos Mexicanos* as their specialty. Such foods as *tacos*, *quesadillas*, *enchiladas*, *burritos* and *tamales* are included in this category. They are regarded not as appetizers but as snacks, although they are often used as a main entree, particularly by those in the lower economic strata. The fact that the majority of Mexican immigrants to the United States have come from this class explains the predominance of *antojitos* in Mexican-American restaurants, and why, when most Americans think of Mexican food, they think of *antojitos*.

Because the use of both *aperitivos* and *botanas* in Mexico fits our perception of appetizers, I have included both in this section. However, because of the real differences between them and *antojitos*, the latter will be found in a separate section. This placement also more accurately reflects our conception of *antojitos* in the United States.

Aperitivos and *botanas* are very special elements of all regional Mexican cuisines. While Mexicans do not go in for desserts nearly to the extent that we do, the opposite is true of appetizers. Although many Mexican appetizers, such as peanuts, *chicharrones* and *tostadas*, are fairly simple, they are used in distinctive ways and with unusual seasonings that make them truly special.

Unless otherwise specified, the appetizer recipes serve four.

TOSTADAS OR TOTOPOS

Tortilla Chips

Tortilla chips, or tostadas, are the appetizer universally provided in Mexican-American restaurants. Often called totopos in the south of Mexico, they are difficult to resist. The problem is that a basket or two takes the edge off one's appetite.

In Mexico, tostadas are used more sparingly. Most restaurants do not serve them automatically. One reason may be that they are not usually as good as those made north of the Border. Mexican tortillas are usually thicker and contain more moisture than ours, making them more difficult to fry properly. Also, thermostat-controlled fryers are not common in Mexico.

Tostadas should by made from the thinnest possible corn *tortillas*, cut into fours, then fried in deep oil at 375-410 degrees until they are crisp. They are ready to serve when they are golden brown and have stopped sputtering. If this does not happen simultaneously, adjust the temperature.

Serve *tostadas* with your favorite *salsas, guacamole* and as a garnish for refried beans. Leftover *tostadas* are used to make *chilaquiles* (see index).

QUESO FLAMEADO

Flaming Cheese

1 lb. mozzarella or farmer's
   cheese, grated
½ lb. chorizo
½ oz. brandy (optional)

Queso flameado, or queso fundido (burned cheese) as it is often called in the south of Mexico, are two names for the same delicious dish. There is really no substitute for queso asadero, or the Mennonite queso de Chihuahua as the principal ingredient. If these are not available, the best substitute for this dish is either mozzarella or farmer's cheese. At restaurants such as the Mexico Típico in Nuevo Laredo, queso flameado is served flaming at the table.

Fry the *chorizo* until well browned. Place the cheese in a flame-proof, medium-sized serving dish. Top with the crumbled *chorizo* and set 6-8 inches under a preheated broiler. Cook until the cheese is melted and bubbling but not browned. While this is cooking, warm the brandy, if used, in a small pan.

When the cheese is ready, remove it from the oven, pour the warmed brandy over the cheese and light it. Set the serving dish, and an ample supply of corn and/or flour *tortillas* and *salsa*, on the dining table. Each person can then spoon individual portions of cheese onto the *tortillas*.

CHILE CON QUESO

❖ ─────────────── ❖

Chile with Cheese

2 Tbs. butter

1 large onion, coarsely chopped

4 green chiles, roasted, peeled, seeded and chopped

1 clove garlic, minced

2 large tomatoes, peeled, seeded and chopped

1 pinch oregano

1 lb. mozzarella cheese, grated

The prevalent—and mistaken—idea of chile con queso probably derives from the variety served at cocktail parties and made with concentrated cheddar cheese soup. The authentic dish from the state of Chihuahua is far superior.

Sauté, over medium heat, the onion, green *chiles* and garlic until they just begin to soften. Add the tomatoes and oregano and continue to cook over medium heat for about five minutes.

Preheat the oven to 425 degrees. Place the cheese in an oven-proof bowl, top with the sautéed vegetables, and bake until the cheese is melted and running into the vegetables but not browned.

Unless it is to be eaten immediately, serve the *chile con queso* in a chafing dish or on a plate warmer. Spoon the cheese mixture on to flour or corn *tortillas*, roll up and eat.

OLIVOS ENCURTIDOS

Cured Olives

1 gallon of ripe green olives
1 gallon of water
3 Tbs. lye
non-iodized salt

Until an old friend of my family, Ray Salcido, brought us some of his home-cured olives, I had always found them too salty and strong-tasting. Ray's olives have a wonderful texture, tender but firm. Their flavor is mild but subtly full, without the overpowering taste of salty brine.

In doing research for this book, I found similarly delicious olives throughout Sonora, where they are sold in bulk from tubs in markets and grocery stores. Ray has kindly allowed me to use his recipe which follows. Please note that this recipe requires lye which, if used improperly, can cause injury. Read and carefully follow all directions on the package.

Olives are ready for curing when they just begin to turn a dark purple.

Dissolve the lye in the water and add the olives. Soak for 24 hours. Rinse the olives with cold water.

Mix 3 heaping tablespoons salt into a gallon of water, add the olives and soak for 24 hours. (Be sure to use non-iodized salt, as iodized salt will spoil the flavor.) Rinse the olives and repeat the procedure twice.

After the final rinsing, prepare another solution of salt water. Place the olives in sterilized jars, fill with the salt water solution, seal and refrigerate.

CHICHARRONES

Fried Pork Rinds

Chicharrones are made from pork rind that is deep fried until crisp and puffy, then lightly salted. One of the favorite Mexican snacks, they are often accompanied by lime halves and Tabasco or a similar sauce.

Chicharrones also are used to flavor frijoles de olla or a la charra, or softened in a sauce as a filling for tacos. In the open-air market in Chihuahua City, there is stall upon stall of large iron cauldrons set over gas fires, filled with bubbling lard in which chicharrones are cooking. The counters are piled high with cooked rinds of all sizes, from about 1 inch to more than 1 foot, priced according to quality and sold by weight.

Chicharrones are not difficult to make if you can find uncooked pork rinds. Cook in oil heated to 350 degrees in a deep fryer until they puff up and become crisp. This takes about 10 minutes. However, *chicharrones* are easier to buy than to make and the commercial products are of acceptable quality.

To serve, place the *chicharrones* on a serving dish, squeeze some lime juice over them and add a few drops of *Tabasco* Sauce. They are also an excellent accompaniment to oysters on the half shell. (See also *Tacos de Chicharrones*.)

CACAHUATES CON CHILE

Hot Peanuts

½ cup cooking oil

¼ cup chiles piquín

8 cloves garlic, peeled (optional)

2 cups raw Spanish peanuts, shelled

salt, to taste

After pepitas and chicharrones, probably the most popular cocktail appetizer in northern Mexico is peanuts. The hot peanuts and garlic peanuts made in Coahuila are truly extraordinary. On trips to the interior, we always stopped at the modest house of an old man in Piedras Negras, across the border from Eagle Pass, Texas. This was the home and factory of the "Hot Peanut Man." We would emerge with brown sacks of delicious, piquant, fresh roasted peanuts. Roasting peanuts is still a cottage industry in that area, although major corporate food companies are now getting into the act with the predictable result—a drop in quality.

Garlic may be added to this recipe, to make hot garlic peanuts. See the next recipe for the full garlic version.

Place the oil, *chile* and garlic in a small pan and warm over low heat for 3 minutes. Do not allow the mixture to approach the simmering point.

Blend the mixture for 2 minutes and let stand for 1 hour. Blend again for 1 minute, then strain into a small glass jar or plastic container.

Next, toss the peanuts with 2 teaspoons of the oil until they are well coated and place them in a large heavy iron skillet.

Place the skillet with the peanuts into an oven pre-heated to 300 degrees and roast them, stirring every 5 minutes for a total of 30 minutes. (The process may take a little longer, depending upon the freshness of the peanuts.)

Remove the skillet from the oven and allow to cool for 30 minutes, when the peanuts will be ready to serve.

CACAHUATES CON AJO

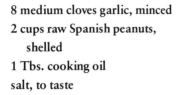

Garlic Peanuts

8 medium cloves garlic, minced
2 cups raw Spanish peanuts,
　　shelled
1 Tbs. cooking oil
salt, to taste

This is a slight variation on the recipe for hot peanuts.

Toss the peanuts with the oil and garlic in a medium-sized, heavy skillet and place in a 300 degree preheated oven for 30 minutes, stirring every 5 minutes.

　　Remove from the oven, pour the nuts into a small bowl and allow to cool for 30 minutes.

　　Salt to taste and serve.

NACHOS

Garnished Tortilla Chips

6 corn tortillas, cut into quarters
4 oz. cheddar or Monterey jack
　　cheese, thinly sliced
24 thin slices of pickled
　　jalapeños

A small restaurant in Piedras Negras, Coahuila, known as Nacho's, claims to have originated the nacho. Regardless of who served the first nacho, its popularity as an appetizer or cocktail snack has spread throughout Mexico and the United States. In this country, we have "nacho-flavored tortilla chips," which do not even approximate the great taste of the real thing.

Deep fry the *tortilla* pieces as for tostadas. Drain on paper towels and arrange on an ovenproof serving dish. Top each fried chip with a slice of cheese and a slice of *jalapeño*.

　　Place the dish of prepared chips about 6-8 inches under a pre-heated broiler for 1 or 2 minutes, or until the cheese is just melted.

NACHOS COMPUESTOS

Special Nachos

Compuesto means "fixed up" and these certainly are. They some-times are called nachos supremos by ambitious restauranteurs.

Do everything as for regular *nachos* except add 1½ cups refried beans and ¾ cup *guacamole* to list of ingredients. Top each *tostada* triangle with: 1 tablespoon refried beans, a slice of cheese and a slice of *jalapeño*. Place the *nachos* under the broiler until the cheese has melted, then remove. Garnish with ½ tablespoon guacamole.

BACON & GUACAMOLE

**¾ lb. bacon, cut extra thick
guacamole (see index)
bolillos (see index)**

This dish makes an appetizer, light lunch or supper that I have often enjoyed in the state of Coahuila. It could hardly be easier to prepare, and the smoke from the fire gives the bacon an extra-special flavor, especially if you use mesquite wood.

Broil the bacon slowly over *mesquite* coals, or charcoal flavored with wood chips, setting the grill about 10 to 12 inches above the fire. The distance from the heat and the cooking time are impor-tant because of the high fat content of the bacon. Serve with *gua-camole, bolillos* and butter for an appetizer. The addition of rice and/or beans makes a lunch or supper dish.

JALAPEÑO EN ESCABECHE

Pickled Jalapeño

1 12 oz. jar
1 Tbs. cooking oil
⅓ cup carrot, sliced
⅓ cup onion, chopped
1⅓ cups jalapeños, sliced or whole
3 garlic cloves, halved
⅔ cup white vinegar
⅔ cup water
1 bay leaf
¼ tsp. oregano
¼ tsp. thyme
¼ tsp. salt
¼ tsp. whole peppercorns

These are the pickled jalapeños that are used on nachos and as a garnish for tacos and beef. Chile lovers enjoy them straight. This recipe makes 1 12-ounce jar, but you can make much greater quantities if you grow your own jalapeños. This is very easy to do and you will find the jalapeños as pleasing to the eye as to the palate.

Place the jar and its lid in a large bowl and cover with boiling water. Place the oil, carrots, onions, garlic and *chiles* in a medium-sized saucepan. Cover and cook over very low heat until the vegetables just begin to soften, about 10 minutes. Add the remaining ingredients, bring to a boil over medium heat and simmer for 1 minute.

While the vegetables are cooking, remove the jar and lid from the water and allow to drain on a clean towel for 5 minutes. Spoon the vegetables into the jar, then add the liquid and cap. Allow to cool, then refrigerate. Pickled *jalapeños* will keep for months if properly sealed and refrigerated.

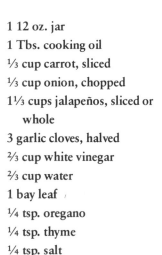

NOPAL

Prickly Pear Cactus

Nopals are the leaves or paddles of the nopal cactus. Nopalitos is the nopal that has been julienned or chopped. The nopal is similar to okra in terms of texture and can be unpleasant if not properly cooked. Nopals are often prepared by char-broiling and boiling. Char-broiled nopal is served with meats and poultry. The boiled version is also served with entrees or as a salad with vinegar and oil. If the leaves have not had their thorns removed you must do so. Then slice off ⅛ inch from the perimeter of the leaf. If charbroiling, place the leaves over coals and cook, turning once or twice for about fifteen minutes. To boil, either julienne or chop coarsely and boil with lots of salt for no less than 25 minutes to remove the viscousness.

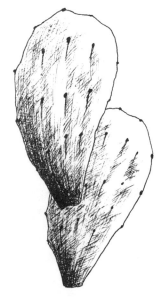

VERDURAS EN ESCABECHE

Pickled Vegetables

½ lb. white salad or red
    potatoes
4 medium-sized squash, such as
    zucchini, crookneck or
    Mexican calabasa
1 small onion, sliced
5 jalapeños, seeded and halved
2 Tbs. olive oil
2 cloves garlic, crushed
½ cup white vinegar
1¼ cups water
2 tsp. oregano
½ tsp. salt
2 bay leaves
⅓ cup jicama sliced thin and
    coarsely chopped

This appetizer, which is very popular in northern Mexico, has a mild and pleasant, rather than a vinegary, taste. Other types of squash or other vegetables may be substituted.

Slice all the vegetables, except the *jalapeños*, to about ⅛ inch thickness. Blanch the potatoes and vegetables until just barely tender. Heat the oil in a large pot over low heat and add the *jalapeños* and onion. Cook, stirring often, until they just begin to soften, 5 to 10 minutes. Add the garlic, cook for 30 seconds, then add the remaining ingredients. Bring the liquid to a boil, then pour into a large ceramic or glass bowl and allow to cool. Refrigerate overnight before serving.

PAN DE MAÍZ

Fried Cornbread

½ cup yellow cornmeal
½ cup all-purpose flour
1 tsp. baking powder
½ tsp. salt
1 Tbs. melted lard or oil
1 egg, lightly beaten
2 pickled jalapeños, seeded and
    minced
2 Tbs. liquid from jalapeño jar
½ cup milk
oil for deep frying

This fried cornbread from Coahuila makes a delicious appetizer when served with guacamole.

Mix the cornmeal, flour, salt and baking powder. Add the lard and egg and mix well. Then add the remaining ingredients to form a thick batter.

Heat the oil to 375 degrees. Deep-fry the bread by immersing in the oil 2 tablespoons of the batter at a time in a large serving spoon. They are finished when puffed, crispy and golden brown. Serve immediately with *guacamole* and *salsa*.

COCTEL DE CAMARONES

Shrimp Cocktail

¾ lb. small to medium-sized
    shrimp
½ cup mayonnaise (preferably
    homemade)
2 Tbs. catsup
1 Tbs. lime juice
¼ cup celery, minced
6 chiles serranos, seeded and
    minced (or quantity to taste)
2 green onions, minced
¼ tsp. salt
½ tsp. pepper, coarsely ground
¼ cup cilantro, chopped and
    loosely packed

As in this country, and especially in Baja California where shrimp are caught daily, they are a favorite cocktail appetizer in Mexico, particularly on the coast of Sonora. This recipe for sauce, from a restaurant in the coastal resort of Mazatlán, is far superior to the thick catsupy sauce commonly used in this country.

Peel and devein the shrimp. Bring a large pot of water to a boil. Using a large strainer, immerse the shrimp in the boiling water until they begin to turn pink. Avoid overcooking. Remove the shrimp and place under cold running water for a minute or two, then transfer them to a bowl of ice water. These last steps are very important because overcooked shrimp lose their fresh taste and texture. To prevent this, cook the shrimp only until they are just done and chill them immediately to stop the cooking process.

Whisk the catsup into the mayonnaise, then add and combine the remaining ingredients except for the *cilantro*. When the shrimp are thoroughly chilled, dry them carefully and toss them with the freshly chopped *cilantro* and the sauce. Serve on small plates or in cocktail glasses.

Soups & Salads

Sopas y Ensaladas

Salads are not as generally enjoyed in Mexico as they are in the United States. In the north, mixed green salads are occasionally served, usually with a vinaigrette dressing, but *guacamole* and Caesar Salad are more common. Soup, however, is another matter. Mexicans make some of the world's finest and most healthful soups. Mexican soups, and those from the north are no exception, are prepared from natural ingredients cooked so as to best capture their essence and flavor.

Most of these soup recipes provide, in themselves, a satisfying light luncheon or supper.

Unless otherwise specified, the soup and salad recipes serve four.

SOPA DE AGUACATE

Avocado Soup

1 medium avocado
1½ cups chicken broth
1 tsp. mild chile powder
¼ tsp. cumin
¾ cup whipping cream
¼ tsp. salt, or to taste
dash cayenne pepper
4 3-inch sprigs of cilantro

I first tasted this soup in a restaurant in the border city of Juarez after a long, hot, dusty drive. It is a refreshing and delicious prelude to a light summer lunch or supper.

Remove the avocado from the skin, chop coarsely and place in the jar of a blender. Add the chicken broth, *chile* powder and cumin and blend until smooth.

Pour the mixture from the blender into a medium saucepan and cook over very low heat until very hot. Do not allow to boil. Pour the avocado mixture into a bowl and allow to cool. Stir in the cream, add the salt and cayenne, and chill thoroughly in the refrigerator.

Pour the soup into individual serving bowls, sprinkle with a little cayenne and garnish with *cilantro*.

SOPA DE AJO

Garlic Soup

3 Tbs. olive oil
6 cloves garlic, crushed
3 slices French bread, crusts
    removed
4 cups chicken broth
salt and pepper

Like many other dishes, garlic soup probably came to Mexico from Spain. It is a tasty accompaniment to the broiled entrees of the north.

Sauté the garlic cloves and bread in the oil over medium heat until they are just browned. Avoid burning. Remove from heat.

Remove the bread, cut into squares of about 1 inch, and return the cubes to the pan. Immediately add the chicken broth, bring to a boil, cover and simmer for 20 minutes, or until the bread has disintegrated and mixed well into the broth.

CALDO DE POLLO

Chicken Soup

1 whole chicken breast

4¼ cups chicken broth

2 chiles anchos

½ tsp. ground cumin

dash pepper, or to taste

½ tsp. salt, or to taste

½ cup tomato, coarsely
chopped

½ cup cooked Mexican rice

2 medium green onions, thinly
sliced

¾ cup zucchini squash,
chopped

1 medium avocado, diced

4 sprigs cilantro

1 lime, quartered

To call this just "chicken soup" is like calling Beef Stroganoff "stew," or Beef Wellington "meat pie." This soup is something special and, with a little planning, provides an excellent light lunch when served with hot flour tortillas and butter. Timing is very important, so that each ingredient is properly cooked.

Place chicken breast in a small pot, cover with water, bring to a boil and simmer until just cooked through. Remove the chicken to a chopping block and allow it to cool. Remove the skin, shred the meat and reserve. Bring the chicken broth to a boil, reduce heat and bring to a simmer. Add the *chiles anchos*, cover and simmer for 8 minutes. Then remove and discard the *chiles*. Add the cumin, the reserved chicken and the rice. Simmer uncovered until the chicken is heated through, about 2 minutes. Now add the zucchini and cook for 3 minutes. Then add the green onions and cook 2 minutes more.

While this is cooking, place ¼ of the chopped tomato in each of 4 soup bowls. After the onions have cooked for 2 minutes, add the salt and pepper and pour the soup into the serving bowls over the tomatoes. Garnish each bowl with the chopped avocado and a sprig of *cilantro*. Serve with hot flour *tortillas* and butter.

CALDO DE QUESO DE SONORA

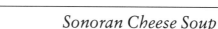

Sonoran Cheese Soup

3 Tbs. butter

½ medium onion, diced

1 medium potato, peeled and
  diced

2-3 green onions, diced

2 medium tomatoes, peeled,
  seeded and chopped

⅔ cup chicken broth or water

1 pint milk, lukewarm

¼ lb. Monterey jack cheese,
  grated

salt, to taste

pepper, to taste

No book on northern Mexican cooking would be complete without a recipe for this rich, creamy soup for which the state of Sonora is famous.

Over medium to medium-low heat, melt the butter and sauté the onion, potato and green onions until they are soft but not brown. Add the tomatoes and sauté over medium to medium-high heat for 3 minutes. Next add the water, bring the soup to a boil, then turn down the heat, and simmer, covered, for 20 minutes.

Remove the cover, turn the heat down very low and add the warm milk and cheese. Stir the soup constantly and cook, without allowing to boil, until the cheese is just melted and incorporated with the soup.

Serve with hot flour *tortillas* and butter.

SOPA DE CALABASA

Squash Soup

2 chicken breasts
5 cups chicken broth
⅔ cup onion, coarsely chopped
2 cups zucchini, coarsely
  chopped
1 cup yellow squash, coarsely
  chopped
1½ cups tomato, peeled, seeded
  and chopped
4 green chiles, peeled, seeded
  and chopped
1½ cups fresh or frozen corn
  kernels
1 tsp. cumin
1 tsp. oregano
¼ tsp. ground black pepper
½ tsp. salt, or to taste

This delicious and filling soup is a meal in itself.

Boil the chicken and remove the skin. Shred when cool and reserve meat. Put the broth in a medium-sized pot and add all the ingredients except the reserved chicken meat. Bring to a boil, turn down heat and simmer, partially covered, for 25 minutes.

Add reserved chicken to pot and heat for 5 minutes more.
Serve with hot flour *tortillas* and butter.

SOPA DE CHILE

Chile Soup

3 chiles anchos, stemmed and
  seeded
3 chiles de árbol or japonéses,
  stemmed and seeded, or to
  taste
1½ quarts mild beef broth
6 Tbs. butter
6 Tbs. flour
2 large or 3 small cloves garlic
3 tsp. oregano
1½ tsp. cumin
salt, to taste
tostadas made from 4 corn tortillas (see index)
6 oz. mild cheddar cheese,
  grated

Place the *chiles*, garlic, oregano and cumin in a blender with 1 cup of the broth and blend for 1 minute. Melt the butter in a large pot, add the flour, and whisk the roux over medium heat until it begins to brown and gives off a nutty fragrance. Remove the pot from the heat and add 1 cup of the broth little by little, whisking well to prevent lumps. Return the pot to the heat and add the remainder of the broth, still taking care to prevent lumping.

Now add the *chile* mixture and bring to a boil. Reduce the heat and simmer, stirring frequently, until the soup begins to thicken (about 15 minutes).

Place equal portions of the cheese and *tostadas* (in that order) into each of four soup bowls. When the soup has reached the desired thickness, ladle it into the bowls and serve immediately.

SOPA DE FRIJOLES NEGROS

Black Bean Soup

½ lb. dried black or turtle beans

2 oz. salt pork, chopped

1 clove garlic

1 tsp. oregano

1 tsp. cumin

1 Tbs. sherry

1 Tbs. lime juice

½ cup sour cream

1 large avocado, chopped

2 green onions, minced

¼ cup cilantro, chopped and
   loosely packed

2 chiles serranos, minced

Black bean soup is not an exclusively northern dish, being popular throughout Mexico. However, this recipe from Chihuahua City is so good that I felt it should be included. The last five ingredients, used as a garnish, contrast beautifully in color with the beans for a stunning presentation.

Wash and place the beans in a bean pot or dutch oven and add water to cover by 2 inches. Add the salt pork and bring to a boil. In a *molcajete* or mortar and pestle, mash together the garlic, oregano and cumin and add them to the beans.

Turn down the heat and simmer covered, until the beans just begin to get tender (about 1½ -2 hours), adding additional water as necessary. Add the sherry and lime juice and continue cooking until the beans are fully tender (about ½ hour). Remove from heat, cool, and then put half of the beans in a blender jar with the cooking liquid. Make sure that none of the salt pork is included. It may be necessary to do this in several stages.

When half the beans and the liquid have been thoroughly puréed, return them to the pot containing the remaining beans. Bring the soup to a boil and simmer about 15 minutes or until it begins to thicken.

Pour the soup into individual serving bowls and garnish with equal amounts of the sour cream, chopped avocado, green onion, *cilantro* and *chiles serranos*. Serve immediately with a lime wedge on the side.

ENSALADA CAESAR

Caesar Salad

3 anchovy filets, or to taste

2 cloves garlic

2 Tbs. green olives, pitted and
sliced

2 Tbs. artichoke hearts,
chopped

5 tsp. lime juice

1 tsp. Worcestershire sauce

pinch salt, or to taste

¼ tsp. coarse black pepper

3 Tbs. garlic oil (see index);
small additional amount to
make croutons

1 egg

3 slices of bread

¼ cup parmesan cheese, grated

8 oz. romaine lettuce

No book on the cooking of northern Mexico would be complete without a recipe for this famous salad. It originated at Caesar's Restaurant in Tijuana during the 1930s. This was an era when, because of Prohibition, many Americans flocked to the border towns for fun — and many creative entrepreneurs developed new ways to supply it. The original recipe has been widely published, but there are several possible variations. This appetizing one from Chihuahua maintains the "flavor" of the original.

In a *molcajete* or mortar and pestle, mash together the garlic and anchovies, transfer to a large salad bowl and add the lime juice. Whisk in the olives and artichoke hearts, then the Worcestershire, salt and pepper. Lastly, add the garlic oil, a little at a time.

To make croutons, brush the bread slices on one side with garlic oil, place on a baking sheet and bake at 350 degrees until they just begin to brown. Turn the bread over, brush with garlic oil and bake until this side begins to brown. Allow the toast to cool and cut into 1-inch squares.

Place the egg in a small bowl or saucepan and cover it with boiling water. After 1 minute remove to a pan of cold water.

Next, break the egg into the salad bowl and whisk it into the mixture. Add the lettuce, parmesan cheese and croutons. Toss well and serve immediately.

GUACAMOLE

Guacamole is the universal salad, appetizer and condiment in northern Mexico. It is made by mashing ripe avocados with lime juice and various herbs and chiles. There are many varieties of avocado in Mexico, but the California Haas is the best (see Ingredients). As an appetizer or salad, guacamole is served with tostadas (fried tortilla chips), or it can be served in a tortilla cup (see following recipe). Experiment with the various combinations of chiles and herbs to find your favorite. Here are a basic recipe and the spicier version I prefer.

BASIC GUACAMOLE

1 medium–ripe avocado

1 Tbs. lime juice

½ medium tomato, coarsely chopped (optional)

1 Tbs. cilantro, loosely packed (optional)

Mash the avocado in a *molcajete* or large bowl with the lime juice until well mixed but not too smooth. Fold in the chopped tomato, and *cilantro,* if used.

SPICY GUACAMOLE

1 medium–sized ripe avocado

1 tsp. chopped, canned jalapeño pepper

1 tsp. liquid from jalapeño can

2 tsp. lime juice

1 Tbs. cilantro, chopped and loosely packed

½ medium–sized tomato, coarsely chopped (optional)

Mix all ingredients as for basic *guacamole.*

TORTILLA CUPS

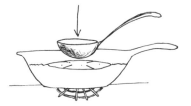

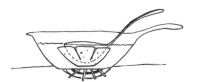

Tortilla cups are corn tortillas fried in the shape of a cup, to be filled with guacamole. They are easy to make and a very attractive addition to any plate. Making the cups requires a 6 or 8 ounce soup ladle approximately 3 inches in diameter, which is used to form the cup.

First, cut the *tortillas* as shown in the diagram. Next, heat oil to 375-400 degrees in a deep fat fryer or dutch oven. Place a cut *tortilla* flat into the oil and immediately press the bottom of the soup ladle's rounded bottom into the middle of the *tortilla*, maintaining pressure until the *tortilla* has wrapped itself around the ladle and is totally immersed in the oil. Hold the ladle in place for about 30 seconds; then remove it, being careful to avoid spilling any hot oil. Repeat this process for as many cups as desired. Allow the now formed cups to continue cooking, turning once or twice with kitchen tongs until they are crisp (about the time they stop sizzling). Remove the cooked cups to drain on paper towels. When cool, store in plastic bags until ready for use. If properly sealed, the bags will keep the cups crisp for up to 24 hours.

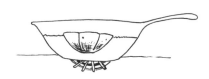

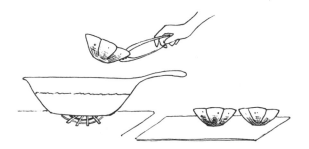

Tortillas & Bread
TORTILLAS Y PAN

Tortillas and *chiles* undoubtedly are the most distinctive and essential elements of Mexican cuisine. The corn *tortilla* is one of the most ancient forms of bread, known in what is now Mexico as long as there has been corn. Even today, in many parts of Mexico *tortillas* are still made as they have been since the advent of Indian culture. Corn is dried and ground into *masa* or dough on stone *metates*. *Tortillas* are then patted out by hand and cooked on a *comal*, the Mexican griddle.

The flour *tortilla*, important to northern Mexican cuisine, is a later variant, following the introduction of wheat and lard by the Spanish.

Today, flour and corn *tortillas* are mostly machine-made, although in some restaurants and in homes with plenty of servants they are still made the superior way, by hand. Whether of flour or corn, hand-made or not, *tortillas* hot from the griddle make the most delicious and versatile of breads.

Because of the popularity of *tortillas, bolillos,* an excellent, more traditional type of bread, are often overlooked. Very much like small French or Italian dinner rolls, they are served with meals, or with such fillings as ham and cheese for delicious *tortas* (sandwiches).

Unless otherwise specified, the tortilla and bread recipes serve four.

TORTILLAS DE HARINA

Wheat Flour Tortillas

2 cups flour
½ tsp. salt
1 heaping ¼ tsp. double-acting
   baking powder
2 Tbs. lard or rendered beef
   suet, or shortening
2 Tbs. butter
⅔ cup very hot water

In most parts of northern Mexico, flour tortillas are preferred to corn tortillas. The tortillas of Sonora are huge, often 15 inches in diameter, and paper-thin. In the state of Coahuila they are often rather small and much thicker, about 4 inches in diameter and ⅛ to ³⁄₁₆ inches thick.

While making a good flour tortilla is easy, making a really great flour tortilla is an art, but one that, with a little practice, is easily learned. Watching an expert is a little like watching a magician: a few quick moves and a small piece of dough becomes a delicate tortilla. Start by following the directions exactly, later experiment with the heat and cooking time, and you soon will be making world-class tortillas.

Note: For the diet conscious, shortening may be substituted for the lard and butter. (See also the section on Nutrition and Northern Mexican Cooking.*)*

Mix the flour, salt and baking powder. Heat the lard and butter or shortening over very low heat. Add to the flour mixture, stirring until well combined.

Beat the hot water into the flour and butter mixture, adding a little at a time until the dough is well combined. Knead the dough for 1 minute, wrap in a dampened towel and allow to rest for 15 minutes. Note: If you have a food processor, combine the dry ingredients and, with the blade in and the machine going, first pour in the butter and lard and then the water, until the dough just forms a ball.

Next, heat an ungreased *comal* or heavy skillet over medium-to-low heat. Lightly flour a smooth counter-top or other work surface. Break off a piece of dough a little smaller than a golf ball (rewrapping the remaining dough to prevent it from drying out), shape it into a ball and flatten slightly. Cover the formed dough with a damp towel. Repeat the process until you have used all the dough. Allow the dough balls to rest for at least 15 minutes or up to 1 hour.

Now, place a dough ball on the lightly floured surface. Push down to flatten it even more and dust the top lightly with flour. Using a small rolling pin (which can be made from a broomstick), roll out the *tortilla* in the following manner: beginning at the center, roll away from you, stopping just short of the edge of the dough. Now, roll back toward yourself, again stopping just short of the edge of the dough. Now, turn the dough ½ turn and repeat the process. Turn the dough and repeat the process once or twice more.

Next, lift the *tortilla*, reflour the work surface, turn the *tortilla* over and repeat the whole process. With a little practice the entire procedure takes only a few seconds. If necessary, turn the *tortilla* and continue rolling until it is ⅛ to ¹⁄₁₆ inch thick and about 6 to 8 inches in diameter.

Next, place the *tortilla* on the ungreased *comal* or skillet and cook until air bubbles begin to form, about 20 to 30 seconds. (At this point, the cooked side should show some browned spots. If it shows some burning the heat is too high; if there is no browning it is too low.) Now, turn the *tortilla* and cook for an additional 20 to 30 seconds, during which time the *tortilla* should continue to puff. Turn again and cook for 10 seconds, or until the *tortilla* stops puffing. Remove the cooked *tortilla* to a *tortilla* warmer or wrap in a towel. Repeat the process for the remaining *tortillas*.

To make bigger or smaller *tortillas* use more or less dough. For example, for *burrito tortillas* use at least triple the dough for each.

TORTILLAS ESTILO SONORA

Sonora Style Tortillas

To make the paper-thin *tortillas* found in Sonora, prepare the dough as for flour *tortillas* but be sure to use a high gluten bread flour. This gives the dough strength and resiliency for the final stretching. Make the dough balls about twice as big as for regular flour *tortillas*, the size of two golf balls, and let them rest a full hour.

Tortilla factories in Mexico first pass the dough through a machine with rollers that looks very much like the hand wringers on old washtubs. This forms the dough into a very thin, round *tortilla*. Finally, and most important, the *tortilla* is stretched by hand into its final shape in much the same way as pizza dough is stretched.

It is helpful to use a *tortilla* press (see Equipment) for the initial stretching because it is difficult for the novice to roll the dough as thin as necessary unless it is just the right consistency and has been allowed to rest sufficiently. I have also used a hand-operated Italian noodle-maker for this preliminary work with great success. The only problem is that it is a few inches shy of the right width. In any case, a satisfactory job can be done by hand.

Make sure that the dough is not too damp or too dry (practice will be your best guide) and sprinkle your work surface and dough ball with flour to keep them from sticking together. Roll the dough as thin as possible. Next, begin stretching it by pulling one side and then the other until you have the desired size and thinness.

In Sonora, *tortillas* are cooked on huge gas-fired griddles. However, few of us have utensils that will accommodate a *tortilla* of 15 or more inches in diameter. Keep the size of your skillet or *comal* in mind when shaping your dough. Finally, cook as for regular flour *tortillas*. Because of their thinness, these *tortillas* cook very quickly and can easily be overdone.

TORTILLAS DE MAÍZ

Corn Tortillas

Corn *tortillas* are much easier to buy than to make and are now available throughout most of the United States. That is the good news. The bad news is that most corn *tortillas* sold in this country are of a decidedly inferior quality. In Mexico, corn *tortillas* are made by soaking dried yellow corn in water overnight, with a little lime added to soften the corn. It is then boiled, ground to a paste called *masa*, shaped into *tortillas* and cooked. Most Mexican corn *tortillas* are made by machine daily in the *tortillerias* (*tortilla* shops), where they are sold fresh. In this country, many commercial *tortillas* are made from corn flour instead of fresh *masa*, which gives an inferior texture. In any case, most of our *tortillas* often are not really fresh, and lack the robust flavor and texture that are necessary to get the most out of Mexican recipes. Our *tortillas*, however, because they usually are thinner and have a lower moisture content, make far better *tostadas* and other items calling for crisp-fried *tortillas*. This is probably why these items are more common here than in Mexico. However, many cities do have *tortillerias* which make their *masa* from corn, rather than from corn flour or *masa harina*.

If good corn *tortillas* are not available where you live, it is well worth your while to buy some of the packaged *masa harina*, such as that made by Quaker, and try making your own. With a little practice you will be pleased with the results. The only equipment you will need is a *tortilla* press, waxed paper and a heavy skillet. Follow the directions on the package and experiment with various levels of heat and timing to find the method that gives the best results.

BOLILLOS

Mexican Rolls

6 ½-7 cups all purpose or, preferably, unbleached high gluten bread flour
2⅔ cups water
1 pkg. active dried yeast
1 Tbs. butter, melted
3 Tbs. sugar
1 Tbs. salt
½ tsp. powdered cinnamon

After tortillas, bolillos are the most popular bread in Mexico. Bolillos are crusty individual rolls with a texture like that of French bread. They are served with entrees, in continental breakfasts, or as tortas (sandwiches).

Mix the yeast in ⅓ cup of the water until dissolved. Allow to sit until bubbly, about 10 minutes. Stir the yeast mixture into the remaining water and add the melted butter.

Place 6 cups of flour in a large mixing bowl. Add the sugar, salt and cinnamon to the flour and stir well. Now make a well in the center of the flour and gradually stir in the liquid mixture, making sure that each addition is well absorbed before adding more.

When the liquid and dry mixtures have been combined into a workable dough, knead it on a well-floured work surface for 8 to 10 minutes until it is elastic. During this process, add enough additional flour to keep the dough from becoming too sticky. Place the kneaded dough into a large bowl that has been lightly greased with butter, turn it to coat with the butter, cover with a damp towel and allow to rise until doubled in volume, 1 to 1½ hours.

After the dough has risen, punch it down and form into oblong rolls about 4 inches long, 2½ inches wide and 1½ to 2 inches high. The rolls should be about the size of half a hotdog bun, but slightly shorter. Place the formed rolls on baking sheets that first have been lightly greased with oil and then dusted with cornmeal. Allow the *bolillos* to rise until nearly doubled in size, 30 to 45 minutes.

Preheat your oven to 375 degrees. Then, using a sharp knife or razor, slash the rolls across the top lengthwise, brush with cold water and place them in the preheated oven. Bake the *bolillos* until the bottoms sound hollow when tapped, 25 to 40 minutes.

Rice & Beans
ARROZ Y FRIJOLES

The preparation of rice in northern Mexico is nearly identical to that in other parts of the country. It is soaked in hot water, dried, then fried in oil until lightly browned. It is then fried with a blended tomato mixture before water is added for the final cooking. The end product is light and dry, with each grain of rice expanded to its maximum size. It can be made in advance and then heated in either a conventional or microwave oven.

Northern bean recipes also are similar to those in other regions, except for one of the most popular versions, Frijoles a la Charra (Beans in the Fashion of the Horsewoman), which originated in the north. This variation uses fried *chiles*, onions, tomatoes and garlic, which are added toward the end of the cooking time. It is the standard accompaniment to *al carbón* entrees.

Unless otherwise specified, the rice and beans recipes serve four.

Arroz Mexicana

Mexican Rice

1 cup long or medium grain
white rice

2 Tbs. cooking oil

1 medium tomato, coarsely
chopped

⅓ medium onion, coarsely
chopped

2 cloves garlic, peeled

1⅔ cups water

1 tsp. salt

1 small carrot, shredded or cut
in julienne strips (optional)

½ chile ancho, minced
(optional)

2 sprigs cilantro (optional)

additional 4 cloves garlic peeled
and left whole (optional)

4 chiles serranos with only the
stems removed (optional)

½ cup frozen peas, thawed
(optional)

This is not the gloppy stuff that we call "Spanish rice," that is often served in Mexican-American restaurants. Authentic Mexican rice is somewhat dry and each grain is fully expanded, while the flavors are distinctive and varied. If prepared with all the optional ingredients, Mexican rice is almost a meal in itself.

Place the rice in a pot, fill with very hot water from the tap and leave for ½ hour. Drain the rice and allow to dry for 15 minutes.

Heat the oil in a heavy pot or dutch oven over medium heat and add the rice. Cook the rice, stirring constantly, until it is golden brown. Avoid burning. While the rice is cooking, place the tomato, onion and two cloves garlic in a blender and blend until smooth.

Turn up the heat under the rice to medium high and add the tomato mixture. Cook the rice and tomato mixture, stirring constantly until nearly all the moisture has evaporated and it just begins to stick to the bottom of the pot.

Now, combine the water and salt and add to the rice. Add and stir in all the optional ingredients used except the peas. Bring the water to a boil, then turn the heat down until it just simmers. This is the last time you should disturb the rice until it is cooked. Continue cooking, uncovered, until all the liquid has evaporated. If you are like me, and just must test the rice toward the end of cooking time, take a narrow pointed knife like a boning knife and gently move aside just enough rice to show if any liquid remains in the pot.

When the rice is done, stir it and add the peas if you are using them. Cover and cook an additional five minutes on the lowest possible heat. Remove the pot from the heat and allow to stand, covered, for ten minutes before serving. (Mexican rice may be prepared well in advance and reheated in a microwave or conventional oven.)

ARROZ BLANCO

White Rice

2 Tbs. cooking oil

1 cup long grain white rice

1¾ cups water or chicken broth

1 tsp. salt

1 clove garlic, minced, or to
    taste (optional)

¼ cup carrot, cut in julienne
    strips (optional)

¼ cup frozen peas, thawed
    (optional)

¼ cup cilantro, chopped and
    loosely packed (optional)

White rice is often served with foods that have a strong or sweet flavor, such as puerco en adobo or chicken mole, and with very mild dishes such as broiled or sautéed fish.

Heat the oil over medium heat in a heavy dutch oven, add the rice and fry, stirring constantly until the rice just begins to color, about 3-5 minutes. Stir the salt into the water or broth and add it to the rice. If you are using garlic and/or carrots, stir them into the rice also at this time.

Bring the water or broth to a boil, then turn the heat down until it just simmers. As with *Arroz Mexicana*, do not disturb the rice after combining all ingredients. Cook until all the liquid either has been absorbed or evaporated. Add the peas and/or *cilantro* at this time, if used, cover the pot and cook for 5 minutes over the lowest possible heat. Remove the pot from the burner, stir the rice well, cover, and allow to steam an additional 5 to 10 minutes.

FRIJOLES

Beans

In northern Mexico the *frijoles* of choice are pinto beans, or occasionally their cousin, pink beans. While I like equally well the black or turtle beans usually served in southern Mexico, I find pintos a more appropriate accompaniment to the robust northern *al carbón* specialties.

Pinto beans are prepared in three basic ways. For *de olla* (of the pot), they are simmered with garlic, cumin, oregano, salt and pieces of salt pork or bacon. For *a la charra* (In the Fashion of the Horsewoman), tomatoes, onions, and *chiles serranos* fried in lard are added toward the end of the cooking period to *frijoles de olla*. Lastly, there is *frijoles refritos* (refried beans), which is *frijoles de olla* mashed and fried in lard. (The substitution of oil for lard is not as successful for these recipes.) *Frijoles de olla* and *a la charra* are most often served with *al carbón* entrees, while *frijoles refritos* usually are served with *antojitos* and *huevos rancheros*.

NOTE: Beans, like stew, are better cooked the day before they are to be served, which allows them to absorb the maximum amount of flavor. Be sure to wash and pick over beans carefully to remove dirt and stones.

FRIJOLES DE OLLA

Beans from the Pot

1 lb. pinto beans, rinsed and
  picked over
2 tsp. cumin
2 tsp. oregano
3 cloves garlic
4 oz. salt pork or 4 strips bacon,
  coarsely chopped
salt to taste
6 cups water

Place beans and water in bean pot or dutch oven. Grind the cumin, oregano and garlic to a paste in a *molcajete* or mortar and pestle and add to the pot with the remaining ingredients. Bring the water to a boil and cover, leaving a small space for steam to escape. Simmer until the beans are tender but not mushy.

Serve with cooking liquid in individual bowls.

FRIJOLES A LA CHARRA

*Beans in the Fashion
of the Horsewoman*

2 large or 3 medium tomatoes,
   chopped
1 medium onion, chopped
3-5 chiles serranos, finely
   chopped, or to taste
2 cloves garlic, minced
   (optional)

Prepare *Frijoles de Olla*. About one–half hour before they are done, sauté the listed ingredients in 3 tablespoons lard or cooking oil.

Cook the ingredients over medium to medium-high until the vegetables are soft but not browned, about 15 minutes. Add them to the beans for the last 15 minutes of cooking.

FRIJOLES BORRACHOS

Drunken Beans

To make this popular dish follow the recipe for *Frijoles de Olla*, substituting 12 ounces of a dark beer for an equal amount of the water.

FRIJOLES REFRITOS

Refried Beans

½ recipe Frijoles de Olla
¼ cup lard or cooking oil
3 cloves garlic
1½ tsp. cumin
¼ medium onion, coarsely
   chopped

Refried beans are usually not refried at all, but fried only once. They are served with entrees or as a filling for tacos and burritos.

Place the garlic, cumin and onion in a *molcajete* or mortar and pestle and grind to a paste. Heat the lard or oil and fry the garlic onion purée until it is soft but not browned and gives off a rich aroma. Traditionally, at this stage the beans and their liquid are poured into the skillet and mashed into the lard or oil with a tool made expressly for this purpose. If you do not have a bean masher, a large slotted spoon will do. I have found that giving the beans a few whirls in a food processor saves considerable effort.

Once the beans have been incorporated into the lard or oil, fry them, stirring constantly, over medium-high heat until they have the consistency of mashed potatoes. Be careful not to let them get dry. If they do, add more liquid.

Serve immediately.

NOTE: As with other recipes in this book, an equal quantity of oil may be substituted for lard. However, the reader is advised that this dish will lose something of its character if the substitution is made.

FRIJOLES MANEADOS

Tied-up Beans

½ recipe Frijoles de Olla

¼ cup lard or cooking oil

3 cloves garlic

1½ tsp. cumin

¼ medium onion, coarsely chopped

2 chiles anchos, soaked in hot water for ½ hour and seeded

2 cups grated asadero, mozzarella or Monterey jack cheese

This recipe, like Frijoles Refritos, is a real northern specialty and, when served with tortillas and some pico de gallo, is a meal in itself.

Place the garlic, cumin, onion and *chiles* in a *molcajete* or mortar and pestle and grind to a paste.

Heat the lard or oil and fry the puréed ingredients for a few seconds over medium heat. Add the beans and some of their cooking liquid and mash them, turning often until all ingredients are well mixed. Fry the beans until they have the consistency of mashed potatoes. Then turn the heat to low, stir in the cheese, and serve.

ENTREES

COOKING AL CARBÓN

Cooking *al carbón* is the heart and soul of northern Mexican cooking. This cooking method derives from the area's ranching heritage and sets it apart from the cooking of southern Mexico. Because many of the recipes in this book are cooked *al carbón*, some background and guidelines for this simple but distinctive cooking method are provided here. (More specific directions will be found in the individual recipes.)

Carbón means "coal," and also refers to cooking over natural wood coals or hardwood charcoal. The best fuel by far for broiling northern Mexican foods is mesquite, which imparts a sweet smokey flavor, or related substances such as huisach or the Hawaiian keawe tree.

Before the introduction of horses and cattle, mesquite was relatively scarce in northern Mexico. Range animals, particularly the horse, regard the mesquite bean (the tree's seed pod) as a delicacy. When lack of rain produces poor grazing conditions, Mexican ranchers will travel long distances to collect truckloads of mesquite beans for their livestock. As the animals moved across the range, they returned the seeds to the earth in a perfect growing medium, and soon the young mesquite trees were everywhere. However, as a mature mesquite tree requires forty gallons or more of water each day, what at first seemed an ideal food supplement became an unpleasant competitor for this scarce resource. Most ranchers on both sides of the Border are happy to see a *leñador* (woodcutter) arrive on their doorsteps, chainsaw in hand, to thin out the mesquite trees. In the state of Coahuila one cannot drive far without seeing a cart or truck laden with mesquite or huisach being transported to homes, to market, or to the *carboneros* (makers of charcoal).

Because of its increasing popularity as cooking fuel, mesquite is now obtainable from markets in most parts of the United States in either wood or charcoal form. If it is not available, oak, hickory or other hardwood will serve. Each gives excellent results, but imparts a different flavor to the food. When cooking with natural woods, I have found that pieces two to three inches in diameter and one foot long will, if properly dried, burn down to coals within thirty minutes. Anything smaller will turn to ash too quickly and larger pieces take considerably longer. The wood can be placed in a portable barbecue, firepit or fireplace. On cold days and nights, there is nothing more relaxing than building a fire and enjoying a glass of wine or a cocktail while the wood burns down to perfect coals. A simple fireplace broiler can be made by using three or four bricks to support the grill from a portable barbecue.

If wood is not available, use a good charcoal made from hardwood rather than petroleum based briquets, which do not provide as much heat and give off an unpleasant odor. For flavoring, add a handful of mesquite chips, sold in many markets, or hickory chips which have been soaked in water for an hour or two. However, never use charcoal for indoor cooking as it emits poisonous fumes.

Cooking time depends on the heat of the coals, the distance of the grill from the fire, the amount of air circulation and the shape of the barbecue or firepit. Experience will be your best guide. When cooking outdoors or in the fireplace, set a second grill somewhat farther from the coals to heat beans, rice, and *tortillas*.

An important difference between the way we and the Mexicans charbroil is that they usually cook their meat over much lower coals for longer periods. I learned this technique years ago on a trip to Muzquiz, Coahuila, where I have a friend who, although a *gringo*, is probably the unofficial mayor of the town. One day he took me out to the foothills of the sierra to a large *palapa*, a sort of grass-roofed pavilion situated beside a creek. Each Saturday this is the home of the Pirañas (piranhas), an unofficial men's club so named because of their affinity for meat. There they gather to spend the afternoon catching up on the week's events, cooking and drinking beer. (Not necessarily in that order).

On a long barbecue constructed of cinder blocks there were large, thin slices of chuck steak cooking over what seemed to be inadequate coals. After about ten minutes one of the men wandered over and turned the meat. This continued over irregular periods. Finally, after 30 minutes or so, a piece of meat was removed, chopped with a cleaver and served with hot flour *tortillas*, *pico de gallo* and a wonderful *salsa*. The meat was tender, and had a smoky, almost buttery taste. The advantages of this type of slow cooking soon became evident. Since precise timing is unnecessary, it does not interfere with socializing; cheaper and more flavorful cuts of meat can be used, and less fuel is required. The only tradeoff is that on thicker, more tender cuts the line between degrees of doneness becomes slightly blurred.

When cooking outdoors with wood or charcoal, or with wood in an indoor fireplace, add some "seasoning" to the coals. Mexican cooks often throw a few pieces of onion and/or garlic, *chiles* and oregano on the coals. This produces a wonderful aroma and adds flavor to the meat. This is the "secret" ingredient in many of northern Mexico's finest restaurants. A good mix is ⅓ medium onion coarsely chopped, 3 unpeeled cloves/garlic, 2-3 whole *jalapeños* or 3-4 *chiles serranos* and 1 tablespoon oregano. Put the mixture on the coals, then put the meat on to cook as soon as the mixture begins to smoke.

If you cannot cook these dishes over wood or charcoal, use a heavy iron skillet with raised ridges, which will create a similar effect. They can also be broiled in the oven or using a gas or electric grill. The results will still be excellent even though you will miss the tangy smoke flavor.

You will note that some of the following dishes are prepared *al pastor* (shepherd style). In many parts of northern Mexico you will see a whole *cabrito* (kid) attached to iron rods being cooked slowly over hot coals at a 45-70 degree angle. Another common sight is food stalls with braziers full of coals where thin pieces of marinated lamb or pork are cooking on vertically placed skewers, with the heat coming from the side (see illustration). As the outer portion of the meat is done, pieces are sliced off and used to fill steaming hot *tortillas*. This is cooking *al pastor*, which derives from the campfire cooking of Mexican shepherds of the north, many of whom are of Basque origin. This style of cooking is par-

ticularly popular in the states of Nuevo León and Tamaulipas.
The best way of duplicating *al pastor* campfire cooking is to use a
barbecue with an electric rotisserie attachment, placed as far
from the coals as possible.

15.   A platter with shishkebobs, *taquitos*, tacos and guacamole illustrates the unusual, mouth-watering combinations found in northern Mexico.

16. As the name implies, *Queso Flameado* is often
served flaming, as an appetizer.

17. This elegant dish of *fajitas* includes grilled *nopals*,
or cactus leaves often served in the State of Coahuila.

18. *Steak Tampiquena*, the ultimate Mexican combination plate, takes some planning but is worth the effort.

19. Shrimp *al mojo de ajo* (in garlic sauce), a favorite
along Mexico's seacoasts, has several variations.

20. Steak and lobster are enjoyed together in northern
Mexico just as they are in the United States.

21.   *Entomatadas*, a type of *enchilada* are delicious, and
the perfect choice for those on a low fat diet.

22.   Northern Mexican meals have a style and elegance
of their own.

Meats
CARNES

Northern Mexico is ranch country and, as one might expect, beef is by far the most popular meat there. However, kid, lamb and pork also are important features of the area's cuisine.

While Mexican beef is not normally as tender as American beef, it is often more flavorful. The reason for this is that most Mexican cattle are grass or range fed instead of being kept in feedlots on a diet of corn and grain. Just as eggs from barnyard chickens that feed on bugs, grass and other natural foods are superior in taste to mass–produced supermarket eggs, so is the flavor of range–fed beef superior. In fact, so many of our meats produced from scientifically fed animals taste so uniformly bland that meat meals in a country such as Mexico, which raises them naturally, are a great treat. In addition to the abundant native grasses, in northern Mexico the cattle graze on wild herbs such as oregano which are said to impart a subtle flavor to the meat.

Mexicans like the strong range–fed beef flavor and will often use less expensive cuts like round and chuck, not so much because they are less expensive as because of their more pronounced flavor. This is illustrated by the popularity of *fajitas* or *arracheras* (skirt steak), which is often preferred over the more expensive tenderloin or sirloin. Skirt steak is difficult to find in some parts of the United States, as most people have never learned how to cook it properly. In fact, in many places it is used for hamburger.

This is not the case in south Texas, where the skirt steak has recently been "discovered" and, in a few short years, has become the best selling steak in most markets. If you are fortunate enough to have a ready supply in your area, it may become one of your favorites as, when properly prepared, it has an incomparable flavor and texture.

Another popular meat which is not frequently found outside northern Mexico is *cabrito* or kid. It is particularly enjoyed in the mountainous state of Nuevo León, whose capital, Monterrey, is also the industrial center of Mexico. This Regio Montana (mountain kingdom) has its own cuisine within the regional cuisine, the most prominent feature of which is *cabrito*. There *cabrito*, almost always less than thirty days old, is cooked *al pastor* (in the manner of the shepherd) rather than *al horno* (in the oven) as it is in other parts of the country. Cooking *al pastor* involves threading the meat, usually the whole kid, on a long metal skewer which is mounted at a 45-70 degree angle over hot coals and turned periodically until the meat is tender on the inside and a crisp, golden–brown on the outside. A barbecue with rotisserie attachment may be substituted, as explained above.

In many parts of northern Mexico, sheep rather than cattle were the first range animals to be introduced. Prominent among the early settlers were sheep ranchers of Basque origin. Basque names such as Elguezabel and Iturria are still common in many places there. While lamb is often cooked *al pastor*, it is more frequently charbroiled and sliced for use in *tacos*.

While pork is not as popular in northern Mexico as it is in southern Mexico, it is still often used. In every region you will find a cook famous for his *carnitas* (literally, little meats). These cooks will arrive at a party or *fiesta* with a huge iron cauldron which is placed on a fire, and into which will be dropped huge chunks of pork and lard. Next to be added are water, spices, fruits and their juices. As the meat cooks over a period of several hours, it is stirred and turned (often with a shovel) until all the moisture has evaporated and most of the fat has been rendered. It is then allowed to cook further until it is crisp and golden on the outside, yet moist and tender on the inside.

Unless otherwise specified, the meat recipes serve four.

CARNE ASADA

Broiled Meat

2 lbs. whole tenderloin, completely trimmed of fat

4-5 medium cloves garlic, peeled

1 tsp. whole black peppercorns, or to taste

½ tsp. cumin

¼ cup olive oil

salt

Carne asada means "broiled meat" and in northern Mexico also means a cookout or barbecue, a picnic in the country where meat is cooked over an open fire.

If you order *carne asada* in a restaurant in northern Mexico, you will usually be served a savory plate of thinly sliced, broiled pieces of tenderloin or sirloin steak accompanied by refried beans, *guacamole*, rice, *pico de gallo* and either flour or corn *tortillas*, or both. The most distinctive thing about this dish is the manner in which the meat is cut. It is trimmed of all fat and then sliced thinly (⅛-¼ inch) with the grain. Elsewhere, when a cut is described as "in the Mexican fashion" or "in the manner of *carne asada*" this is what is meant. These steaks, because they are so thin, must be broiled very quickly over the hottest possible coals to achieve a rare or medium-rare state. This is especially true for Steak Tampiqueña and steak and *enchiladas* (see index) which are served on a sizzling hot plate. For these dishes, broil the meat on one side only, if you like it rare, then place it uncooked side down on the heated plate, which completes the cooking.

When making *carne asada*, allow about ½ pound of meat per person and serve with refried beans and/or rice, *rajas* (see index), *guacamole*, *pico de gallo* and hot *tortillas* or *bolillos*. Better yet, take the time to prepare Steak Tampiqueña, which is the ultimate Mexican combination plate.

The following recipe for *carne asada* is sure to become one of your favorites, especially if you like garlic.

If the tenderloin is more than about 8 inches long, cut it in half. Slice it lengthwise, with the grain, into slices about ¼ inch thick.

Place the garlic, pepper, cumin and olive oil in a *molcajete* or mortar and pestle and grind until the garlic is puréed and the spices pulverized. Toss the oil mixture with the sliced meat and marinate in the refrigerator for at least 3 hours or overnight.

Broil the meat very close to a very hot fire to the desired degree. Add salt to taste and serve as suggested above.

AGUJAS

Thin Chuck Steak

2½ lbs. bone-in, chuck steak,
    cut no more than ½ inch
    thick
juice of 3 or 4 limes
salt

Agujas are thin steaks, easily prepared, and a true northern Mexican dish. The protracted cooking time over low heat makes this a favorite dish at carne asadas or cookouts, where precise and demanding cooking processes which would interfere with socializing are not favored. Even if you usually prefer steak rare or medium–rare, you will soon become addicted to the smoked, almost buttery consistency of this well–done meat. The secret of this dish is that when high fat content meat cooks over a low fire it will be well charred and impregnated with smoke without drying out.

Pound the steak to about ¼ inch thickness, using the side of a heavy cleaver. Pour the lime juice onto the meat, salt it well and marinate in the refrigerator for 1-3 hours.

Broil the meat on a grill set at least 6-8 inches away from a slow mesquite fire until very well done. Turn the meat every five minutes, for about 20 minutes.

T-BONE STEAK

T-bone and porterhouse steaks are as popular in Mexico as they are in the United States. A T-bone is actually a sort of combination steak, being a New York cut on one side of the bone and a filet mignon on the other.

When broiling T-bones, be sure that the meat is a good distance from the coals. This cut has more fat than any other except the ribeye, and is therefore susceptible to catching fire. Mexican butchers tend to leave a great deal more fat untrimmed from the steak than we do, often as much as 2 inches. A steak trimmed in this manner and served on a sizzling iron platter is an impressive sight.

The T-bone is usually served with french fried potatoes, *frijoles a la charra*, or both.

The thinnest possible cut of T-bone will weigh about ½ pound, but any size up to 1½ to 2 pounds is manageable. An hour or two before cooking, brush the steaks with garlic oil and add a few grinds of pepper. Broil over hot coals being careful to keep the steaks far enough from the coals to prevent burning.

FAJITAS OR ARRACHERAS

Skirt Steak

This cut of meat is called fajitas in Texas and along the Border in Mexico. Further south, it is usually known as arracheras. While still not favored in many parts of the United States, the skirt steak, which a few years ago was used only for hamburger, is becoming more popular here. As was mentioned earlier, this is now the preferred steak in many parts of Texas where there are almost weekly fajita cookoffs. I also have seen fajitas on restau-

rant menus in California and New York. We are beginning to learn what the Mexicans have known for years: that, when properly cooked, the skirt steak can be almost as tender as any other cut and always will be more flavorful.

Fajitas are served whole with rice, refried beans and *guacamole*, or sliced as a filling for Tacos de Fajitas. For the latter, the meat is often brought sizzling and steaming to the table on a large iron plate or skillet, a dramatic presentation that makes it a winner in restaurants. For Tacos de Fajitas, broil the meat to one degree less than desired. For example, if you want it medium rare, broil it until just rare. Then slice the meat into bite-size pieces. While you are doing this, heat a heavy iron skillet over high heat for just a few minutes to avoid damaging it (or yourself, if the heat should cause it to break). Just before serving, transfer the meat to the hot skillet and add the juice of 2 to 3 limes. This is what creates the steam and sizzle. Place the skillet, set on a trivet or other heat-resistant item, on the dining table. Set out bowls of *guacamole*, *pico de gallo*, your favorite sauce and plenty of hot *tortillas*.

Another popular variation is Fajitas Encebollada (Fajitas with Onions). For this variation, thinly slice one large onion and fry in 1 tablespoon of olive oil, peanut oil or lard until very brown, about 20 minutes. During the last 10 minutes add four small limes, halved. Add the meat and the cooked onions and lime halves to the heated iron skillet at the same time and mix well just prior to adding the lime juice.

To be completely tender, *fajitas* should be marinated for a few hours or overnight prior to cooking. The marinade for Chicken Shishkebob is a good choice, especially if ½ tablespoon of cornstarch, which helps the tenderizing process, is added. An alternate marinade can be made with ¼ cup lime juice mixed with ½ tablespoon of garlic powder and ¼ teaspoon of salt, black pepper and onion powder to taste. As a last resort, if you are short of time, or if the meat does not appear well aged, a commercial meat tenderizer may be used.

Note that, while *fajitas* are thinner than most of the steaks we usually use, they take somewhat longer to cook.

Allow about ½ pound of skirt steak per person. (See also Tacos de Fajitas.)

BIFTEC RANCHERO

Steak with Ranchero Sauce

4 6-8 oz. New York or ribeye
   steaks

3 Tbs. lard or olive oil

1 medium onion, coarsely
   chopped

2 cloves garlic, minced

4 green onions, coarsely
   chopped

1 chile poblano, chopped; or
   substitute a chile anaheim or
   bell pepper

2 chiles serranos, finely sliced

4 medium tomatoes, seeded and
   coarsely chopped

½ cup cilantro, chopped and
   loosely packed

This version of Biftec Ranchero is a real northern specialty. The tomatoes, onions, and chile sauce also are used for Pork Ranchero and Eggs Ranchero. Steak Ranchero is one of those dishes that require fresh, not canned, ingredients. Any good steak can be used, but New York cut or ribeye are preferable.

If broiling the steaks over a fire, start the fire and then prepare the ingredients for the sauce. When the coals are about 15 minutes from being ready, prepare the sauce.

Heat 2 tablespoons of the lard or olive oil in a large heavy skillet. Add the onion, garlic, green onions and chiles. Cook over medium-high heat, stirring frequently until they are just soft but not browned, about 10 minutes.

Add and melt the remaining 1 tablespoon of lard or add 1 tablespoon of olive oil, and the tomatoes, stirring well to combine with other ingredients. Reduce the heat to medium and cook, stirring often, until all the liquid has evaporated. Now broil the steaks to the desired degree and place on individual serving plates. Remove the sauce from the heat, stir in the *cilantro* and spoon the sauce over the steaks. Serve with refried beans and rice.

BIFTEC A LA PARILLA

Panbroiled Steak

4 8 oz. T-bone or porterhouse
steaks (the porterhouse has
the larger filet)

Although charbroiling is by far the most popular method of cooking steaks in most parts of northern Mexico, many people, there as here, prefer their steaks panbroiled for reasons of convenience or taste. In panbroiling, the meat is cooked in a heavy skillet over medium to medium–high heat (depending on thickness), using just enough fat to keep it from sticking. The best source of fat for this purpose is rendered suet from the fat trimmings of the steaks. This is done while the skillet is heating. Biftec a la Parilla is particularly popular in the state of Chihuahua, where it is served with the same accompaniments as steaks al carbón. In Chihuahua City and Juaréz, the steaks often are cooked and served in individual iron or steel plates that have wooden bases made especially for this purpose. This creates a spectacular, sizzling presentation. Heat resistant gloves should be used for serving, and care should be taken to avoid burns from the popping fat.

The following recipe is for T-bone or porterhouse steaks which, because of their fat content, are particularly easy to panbroil. The same is true for ribeyes. The instructions may by applied to other cuts of beef and to pork. The following recipe calls for 8 ounce steaks, which is about as thin as it is practical to cut a T-bone. In Mexico this thin cut is preferred, I suspect, because it is so economical. Another reason I like the panbroiled method and using this smaller cut is that grilling creates a much "heavier" product than broiling. I find that an 8 ounce serving provides the optimum portion conducive to later comfort.

Trim the steaks of excess fat, place 2 to 3 ounces of the fat in a large iron or other heavy skillet over medium–high heat. Using kitchen tongs, turn the fat pieces frequently as they begin to sizzle to prevent them from burning. When the skillet is very hot and the rendered fat is beginning to smoke, remove any remaining pieces of fat and add the steaks. Cook them about 1½ minutes on each side for rare steak, more for other degrees of doneness, and serve immediately with guacamole, beans, rajas and rice.

If you have individual steel or iron cooking plates with wood bases, cook the steaks individually in the plates. Then, after adding the accompaniments, use heat resistant gloves to set them in their insulating wooden bases on the table. For variation, heat the individual plates in the oven at 350 degrees, cook the steaks in the large skillet, place them on the hot plates and serve as above. If using either of these techniques, remember that the steaks will continue to cook long after they are served. To avoid an overdone steak, cook as suggested above on one side and then turn and cook 15 seconds on the other side before placing, lightly-cooked side down, on the serving plates.

BIFTEC PIMENTAL

Mexican Style Pepper Steak

1 cup red, ripe chile anaheim, peeled, seeded and chopped.
3 red bell peppers, seeded but not peeled, and sliced into thin strips, may be substituted
1 clove garlic, minced (optional)
2 Tbs. butter
black pepper, to taste (to be added if using bell peppers)

Biftec pimental is steak topped with strips of seeded and peeled chiles that have been sautéed in butter. A perfectly ripe, red chile anaheim is usually used. The flavor of the ripened chile is more rounded and mellow than when it is green, and it is almost sweet. These ripe chiles are rarely available in the United States. If you cannot grow your own, substitute a good red bell pepper. This way of serving steak is common in Chihuahua where steaks are usually panbroiled instead of charbroiled. However, either method may be used for this dish.

Choose your favorite steak: T-bone, ribeye and New York are good choices. Cook either *al carbón* or panbroil and serve topped with the listed ingredients.

Heat the butter in a medium–sized skillet over medium heat. Add the garlic, if used, and then add the pepper. Sauté the pepper until soft and use as a topping for the steak.

STEAK TAMPIQUEÑA

1 lb. filet steak, carved in the Mexican fashion (see Carne Asada)

½ lb. shredded meat for tacos (chicken also is often used)

2 dozen tortillas (only 1 dozen are needed, but allow for mistakes)

1 recipe Mole Sauce

Guacamole, made with 2 avocados

1½ cups refried beans

1 recipe Mexican Rice

1 recipe Rajas

shredded lettuce or cabbage

chopped tomatoes

Steak Tampiqueña is the aristocrat of Mexican combination plates and is a favorite restaurant meal, particularly in northern Mexico. It consists of a small filet cut in the Mexican fashion (see Carne Asada) and several other items, usually an enchilada, taco, refried beans, rice, guacamole and rajas (strips of fried green chile and onion). The prospect of a good filet Tampiqueña dinner has often tempted me to spend a weekend in Mexico. Two of the best versions may be found at the Mexico Típico restaurant in Nuevo Laredo and Martino's restaurant in Ciudad Juarez. Since the recipes for all of the Tampiqueñas' accompaniments are given elsewhere in this book, only the final preparation or assembly is described here. It takes a little planning and practice to get the timing right, but the result is well worth the effort.

Using the meat shredded as for tacos, make four Mole Enchiladas (or substitute cheese of your choice) and place on an ovenproof plate in a 375 degree oven for 8 to 10 minutes. While this is cooking, make four *guacamole* cups and fill them with the *guacamole*. Make *tostadas* from 2 *tortillas*, as a garnish for the beans. Next, make 4 shredded meat tacos with either crisp or medium-fried *tortillas*.

Remove the plates with the *enchiladas* and arrange the *tacos*, *rajas*, *guacamole* cups, refried beans and rice as shown in the diagram. Place two *tostadas* in each serving of beans.

Using a very hot fire, broil the steaks very quickly, about 1½-2 minutes on the first side, and 1 minute on the second (as it will be placed against the sizzling hot plate) and set on the plate. Garnish the plates with the lettuce or cabbage and tomatoes and serve, using hot dish holders. Be sure the table is protected with heat-resistant place mats.

COSTILLAS DE RES

Beef Short Ribs

THE MARINADE

4 chiles anchos

4 chiles japonéses

1 Tbs. oregano

4 cloves garlic

1 Tbs. cumin

⅓ cup mild red wine vinegar

⅓ cup cooking oil

½ tsp. salt

This dish makes a hearty addition to any carne asada (barbecue) and also is delicious and filling by itself. As the ribs are very thick and fatty, keep the grill well away from the coals to prevent burning on the outside.

Score 4 pounds of beef short ribs by slicing them, at ¼ inch intervals, one way and then the other, as though you were trying to set up a crossword puzzle across the fatty tops. Then marinate, refrigerated, for 2 hours.

To prepare the marinade, remove the seeds and stems from the chiles, soak them in hot water for 10 minutes, and place them in a blender with the remaining ingredients. Blend for 60 seconds. If the mixture is a little too thick to blend satisfactorily, add a little water and continue to blend.

Broil the ribs for 30-45 minutes, setting them far enough from the coals to prevent flareups and burning on the outside.

Good accompaniments are hot corn *tortillas*, *pico de gallo* and any of the *jalapeño* sauces. Slice the meat into small pieces and wrap with the other ingredients in the hot *tortillas*.

CARNE GUISADA

Beef Stew

2 lbs. very lean round steak or
   stew meat, cut in 1–inch
   pieces
1½ Tbs. flour
¼ cup lard or cooking oil
1 tsp. salt
1 Tbs. oregano
½ tsp. cumin
4 cloves garlic
3 chiles anchos, stemmed and
   seeded, but left whole
3 to 6 chiles japonéses or de
   árbol, stemmed and seeded
¼ cup tomato sauce

Carne guisada is a delicious Mexican style stew that somewhat resembles Texas-style chili. Carne guisada has recently become very popular in south Texas, where it is made with potatoes, carrots and celery and thickened with flour toward the end of the cooking process, very much as we do with our leftover stews. Carne guisada is usually eaten with flour tortillas.

The following is an authentic northern Mexican recipe which I picked up while participating in a cattle drive on a friend's ranch. There it was made with airmailed chiles and neighbor's meat.

My friend flew me to the cow camp, where he also delivered some supplies. The unhappy cook pointed out that the chiles had been forgotten. Later in the day my rancher friend returned and, circling just above us, dropped several well wrapped bags of chiles. As I watched him prepare the stew, I asked the cook what cut of meat he was using. He replied with a grin "Carne de vecino," which literally means "neighbor's meat." He quickly assured me that he was not a rustler, but had traded some dry provisions to the neighboring ranch foreman for the steer.

Heat the lard or oil over medium heat in a heavy iron pot or dutch oven. Place the beef and flour in a paper bag and shake until the beef is well coated. Mash the garlic, oregano and cumin together in a *molcajete* or mortar and pestle.

When the lard or oil is hot, add the beef and cook, stirring continuously to prevent scorching, until it is well browned. Pour off any excess lard or oil and add enough water to just cover the meat. Then add the remaining ingredients.

Bring the mixture to a boil, cover and simmer 1½ hours, or until the meat is very tender and most of the cooking liquid has evaporated. (There should be very little gravy.) If necessary, add more water. If it is too watery, remove the cover and continue cooking until the proper consistency is reached.

Serve with flour *tortillas* and your favorite sauce.

MILANESA

Breaded Veal Cutlet

1 lb. veal, tenderloin or tender-
ized round steak, sliced ⅛
inch thick

2 eggs beaten with 3 Tbs. water
and salt and pepper to taste

flour

bread crumbs

cooking oil

You will find this dish on the menu of almost any good restaurant in northern Mexico. Since veal is not often used in Mexico, tenderloin sliced thin as for carne asada or round steak, pounded to tenderize it, is commonly substituted. As with many other northern Mexican foods, particularly the steaks, it is not so much the entree of breaded veal that makes this dish special, but the choice of items which accompany it. Milanesa is usually served with refried beans and/or arroz mexicana, rajas, or fried strips of chile, onion, and sometimes squash and guacamole, and a lime half. This combination is delicious and uniquely Mexican.

Dip the pieces of meat (veal if you can afford it) into flour and shake off the excess. Next, dip the floured meat into the egg mixture and coat with the bread crumbs. Refrigerate the meat for at least one hour.

Heat ¾ inch of cooking oil in a heavy skillet until it is very hot, or until just before it begins to smoke. Cook the meat for about 20 to 30 seconds on each side, or until done. The trick is to see that the coating is nicely browned and the meat inside still moist and tender.

Serve as suggested above.

CORDERO AL PASTOR

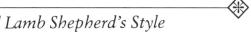

Roasted Lamb Shepherd's Style

1 leg of lamb

MARINADE

1 tsp. chile piquín

5 cloves garlic

½ tsp. oregano

6 fresh mint leaves or ½ tsp. dried

½ tsp. mild chile powder

½ tsp. salt

½ tsp. pepper

¼ cup cilantro, chopped and loosely packed

3 Tbs. minced onion

¼ cup olive oil

2 Tbs. lime juice

As previously stated, the best way to duplicate *al pastor* cooking is to use a barbecue with a rotisserie attachment. If you have this equipment, ask the butcher to bone and tie the lamb so it can be threaded onto the skewer.

To make the marinade, grind all the ingredients into a paste in a *molcajete* or mortar and pestle. Rub the paste onto the lamb and marinate covered in the refrigerator overnight.

If using a barbecue with a rotisserie, cook as far from the coals as possible until done, 45 minutes to 1¼ hour per pound. If you do not have the rotisserie, leave the bone in the lamb and use an electric or charcoal smoke cooker, following the directions for leg of lamb; or bake in a 350 degree oven for 30 to 40 minutes per pound.

If you are using the meat for *tacos*, slice it diagonally into bite-size pieces and serve with *frijoles de olla* or *a la charra*, *pico de gallo*, your favorite table sauces and plenty of hot *tortillas*. Alternatively, serve as a main meat course with rice and/or beans, as above.

ALBONDIGAS EN SALSA DE CHILE

Meatballs in Chile Sauce

THE MEATBALLS

2 slices stale or dried bread,
   crumbled

2 small eggs

⅓ cup minced onion

2 chiles chipotles or anchos,
   seeded and finely chopped

¼ cup uncooked rice

1 tsp. salt

¼ tsp. pepper

1½ lbs. ground beef

⅓ cup cooking oil

THE SAUCE

4 Tbs. butter

3 Tbs. flour

1 medium onion, thinly sliced

2 medium carrots, cut in
   julienne strips

3 cups beef broth

4 tomatoes, peeled, seeded and
   finely chopped

1 clove garlic

¼ tsp. cumin

½ tsp. oregano

2 chiles chipotles or anchos,
   seeded and finely chopped

Several kinds of chiles may be used for this dish. I prefer either the canned chiles chipotles or chiles anchos. If neither is available, use chile powder.

To make the meatballs, mix well all the ingredients except the cooking oil. An electric mixer or food processor will do this efficiently. Form the mixture into 1-1½ inch balls. Heat the cooking oil in a large, heavy pot or dutch oven over medium-high heat. Add the meat balls and fry, turning often until they are well browned. Then remove them and drain on paper towels while you prepare the sauce.

Pour off the remaining oil and return the pot to the burner. Turn the heat to low and melt the butter. Add the onion and fry, stirring often until it becomes soft and translucent. Add the carrots and flour and cook, stirring often, for about three minutes, being careful not to let the flour burn. Remove the pot from the heat and add the broth a little at a time, stirring well after each addition. When about half of the broth has been added, return the pot to the burner and add the remaining broth in a stream while stirring constantly.

Next, crush the garlic, cumin, oregano and *chiles* in a *molcajete* or mortar and pestle and add them and the tomatoes to the pot. Add the reserved meatballs and bring the liquid to a boil. Then turn the heat to low or medium-low and simmer for 30 minutes or until the sauce is thickened. Add a little salt to taste and serve with Mexican or white rice.

ALHAMBRES DE CARNE DE RES

Beef Shishkabobs

½ cup red wine vinegar
¼ cup dry vermouth
3 Tbs. cooking oil
5 cloves garlic, minced
½ tsp. salt
½ tsp. black pepper
1 Tbs. unflavored meat
    tenderizer

In northern Mexico, Beef Shishkebobs are usually made from the tenderloin or filet and are normally not marinated. Because of the cost of this cut in the United States, I usually substitute sirloin which, when marinated, is sufficiently tender.

BEEF

Use 1½ pounds sirloin steak, trimmed of all fat and cut into pieces approximately 1½ inches square and ½ inch thick. If using a marinade, soak the meat, refrigerated, overnight, or for at least 3 hours.

MARINADE

Use the marinade for Chicken Shishkebob or any other marinade you like, such as this one, that does not contain soy sauce or a sweetener.

Mix all ingredients well.

SHISHKABOBS

Follow the directions for Chicken Shishkabobs, using the same ingredients in the same order.

FRITADA DE CABRITO

Kid in its Blood

1 small kid (under 9 lbs.)
3 Tbs. olive oil
blood from the kid
4 chiles anchos
½ tsp. pepper
½ tsp. cumin
½ onion, chopped
salt, to taste

This and the following recipe, for Barbacoa are not for the squeamish. Also, their major ingredients are not normally available to most of us. However, both dishes are important in the northern Mexican cooking tradition. I have tried both and, if you can banish disquieting mental images, and they are properly prepared, they are delicious.

This recipe was given to me my friend Rogelio Chavarria Montemayor of Muzquiz, Coahuila.

Remove the meat from the bones of the kid and cut into bite-sized pieces. Sauté the meat in the oil in a heavy pot or dutch oven over medium heat until just browned.

In a separate pan, mix the blood with 1 cup water and heat over very low heat for 10 minutes, stirring occasionally.

Seed and devein the *chiles* and blend for 1 minute, using just enough water to make a purée.

When the meat is browned, add the *chile* mixture, the blood mixture to cover the meat (add more water, if necessary), then the remaining ingredients. Simmer covered until the meat is tender. If the "gravy" is not thickened, remove the cover and simmer to desired consistency.

Fritada is served with hot *tortillas*.

BARBACOA

Barbecued Head of Cow, Goat or Sheep

1 cow, goat or sheep's head, skinned but with nothing else removed.

This is a weekend dish in the north of Mexico. Proper preparation requires a special pit. It is often prepared by meat markets on weekends and during fiestas.

First, a large quantity of *mesquite* is burned down to coals, half of which are placed in a pit lined with volcanic rock or fire brick and several times larger than the head.

The head is wrapped in several layers of wet burlap and a wire placed around it to facilitate its later removal. The package is then lowered onto the coals. The remaining coals are now placed on top of the head. A cover, usually made of clay or iron, is fitted over the head but well below the ground surface. Earth is piled over the cover and tamped down to seal the pit and make it air-tight.

The process usually is begun in the afternoon or evening and the head is allowed to cook until morning (12-18 hours). After the head has been lifted from the pit, the brains, tongue, cheeks and other parts considered edible are removed and served with hot *tortillas* and sauce.

This method of cooking produces a unique smokey taste. In the United States, Hispanic restaurants and *tortilla* factories often make *Barbacoa* by steaming the heads in large kettles over water. I do not recommend that version.

CARNITAS

Pork Tidbits

2 lbs. boneless pork shoulder,
   cut into ½ to 1 inch pieces

2 tsp. cumin

2 tsp. oregano

4 cloves garlic

4 chiles piquíns

½ tsp. salt, or to taste

water

Carnitas are from the south, notably the state of Michoacán. However, they also are enjoyed in the north, particularly at bar-becues and fairs. Carnitas are usually made by placing very large cuts of pork, a lot of lard or oil and some water in huge cauldrons set over coals or gas jets. The meat is cooked for a long time until the exterior is crisp and the meat is nearly falling apart. Because of these cooking requirements, Carnitas are usually not fixed at home. I also find the amount of lard used a bit unpalatable.

However, this recipe from the north takes only a short time to prepare and requires no added fat if you use a fatty cut of meat, such as the shoulder. Country–style spareribs also work very well, especially if you can get them cut into sections about three inches long. I find this version is just as crisp and flavorful as the more traditional Carnitas.

Place the cut–up meat in a large, heavy skillet and add just enough water to cover. Grind together the cumin, oregano, garlic and chiles in a *molcajete* or mortar and pestle and add to the skillet with the salt.

Bring the liquid to a boil and reduce the heat to low. Simmer until all the liquid has evaporated. At this point the meat should be very tender and enough fat should have been rendered to allow it to fry without sticking. If the meat is not yet tender, keep adding more water and cook until it is. If there is not enough fat in the pan, add some lard or cooking oil. Increase the heat to medium and continue cooking, stirring constantly until the meat is brown and crisp on the outside, but still tender and moist on the inside, 5 to 10 minutes.

Serve Carnitas with rice or use for *tacos*.

CARNITAS DE JUGO

Carnitas with Juice

Follow the basic recipe for Carnitas, but add 1 cup of orange juice or pineapple juice, or a combination of both, before covering the meat with water. Also, keep the heat low for the final frying. The sugar from the juices easily burns, imparting a bitter taste if it does.

Serve Carnitas de Jugo with flour *tortillas*, charbroiled green onions, rice and your favorite sauce.

PUERCO EN ADOBO

Pork in Adobo Sauce

6 chiles anchos, stems and seeds
   removed
1½ tsp. sugar
⅓ cup cider vinegar
⅔ cup chile water
⅓ cup onion, chopped

Pork adobo is common to Spanish-speaking countries from Spain to the Philippines, but these dishes have few similarities apart from using pork. Each area's variation on the recipe is influenced by the availability of ingredients and local tastes.

Following the recipe for Carnitas de Jugo, when all the liquid has evaporated add the *adobo* sauce and simmer the pork over low heat, stirring often, for 20 minutes.

Place the *chiles* in a bowl, pour hot water over them and soak for 20 to 30 minutes. Place the softened *chiles* in a blender, add the remaining ingredients and blend at high speed for 1 minute.

Serve with white rice.

CORTADILLO

Diced Beef Sautéed with Vegetables

1½ lbs. lean, thinly sliced beef, such as "breakfast steaks"

¼ cup lard or olive oil

4 tomatoes, seeded and coarsely chopped

1 large onion, coarsely chopped

2 small chiles poblanos, anaheims or green peppers, coarsely chopped

4 chiles serranos, halved, seeded and thinly sliced across the width

½ tsp. salt

¼ cup cilantro, chopped and loosely packed

This is a truly traditional northern dish, dating back to the seventeenth century. It combines regional ingredients in a simple manner, but one which produces a surprisingly complex blend of flavor and texture. As its name, deriving from the verb cortar, "to cut," suggests, it is made by cutting up ingredients, which are then fried in a manner similar to Chinese style stir-frying. Cortadillo is served in its juices or somewhat thin gravy, accompanied usually by refried beans and corn or flour tortillas to "clean" the plate. It is not often found on restaurant menus, where it is sometimes called Biftec a la Mexicana, but is nearly always available on request. Cortadillo is particularly favored in Coahuila and Nuevo León as an early morning "fortifier" after a bout in the cantinas.

Note: Cortadillo can be cooked with less lard or oil than recommended below, but with considerable loss of flavor and texture.

Melt the lard or heat the olive oil in a heavy skillet over high heat and add the beef. Fry until browned, stirring often. Add the onion and *chiles* and continue frying until they begin to soften.

Turn the heat to medium–high and add the tomatoes. Continue frying until they are soft and about ¾ cup of gravy or juices has been rendered. If there is not enough juice, add a little hot water. Just before serving, stir in the salt and *cilantro*.

Serve with rice or refried beans and hot flour or corn *tortillas*.

COCHINITA PIBIL DEL NORTE

Pit-cooked Pork, Northern Style

3½ lbs. boneless pork loin roast

MARINADE

2-3 chiles anchos, seeded and
deveined

2 chiles de árbol, seeded and
deveined

¾ cup orange juice

3 cloves garlic

½ Tbs. oregano

¾ tsp. salt

½ tsp. black pepper

juice of 1 small lime

Cochinita píbil is a famous dish from the Yucatán, a long way from northern Mexico. This recipe is included not only because it is excellent, but also as an example of the many recipes from other regions which have become a part of the northern cuisine.

A few years ago I stopped at a small roadside stand in the village of Magdalena, Sonora. As I was not familiar with the area, I picked the one open air stall of many that seemed to be the busiest. The owner was carving delicious looking slices from a large piece of smoked pork which had obviously been marinated. The pork was cooked in a huge pit barbecue which sat beneath a thatched roof. The sliced pork was placed on flour *tortillas* that had been heated over the barbecue. Sliced green onions, which had also been charbroiled, and a spoonful of *guacamole* topped the pork.

This *taco*, with the smoky texture and flavor of the pork, was unusually tasty. When the lunch crowd had thinned, I asked the stall owner about the meat. He said it was the Yucatán specialty, but I was pretty certain that there was no *achiote*, which gives the Yucatán dish its character, in the marinade. He said I was right, that since *achiote*, the ground seed of the *anatto*, was difficult to find he used other ingredients. These he kindly identified for me. After some experimentation, I was able to duplicate the flavor of his *tacos*, which is different from the classic Yucatán version but just as good, if not better.

This dish is best cooked in a water–smoker or other barbecue that cooks with indirect heat (not directly over the coals), but also may be prepared on a rotisserie or in the oven.

Place all marinade ingredients in a blender and blend at high speed for 1 minute. Place the pork and marinade in a noncorrosive bowl and marinate in the refrigerator for at least 3 hours or overnight.

Smoke the meat in the barbecue for 45 minutes to 1 hour per pound, or bake at 350 degrees until a meat thermometer registers 150 degrees.

Use for *tacos*, as described above, or as a main course with rice or beans.

COSTILLAS DE PUERCO

Pork Ribs

4 lbs. pork spare or
country–style ribs
marinade for beef ribs, substituting cider vinegar for
wine vinegar

These are prepared in much the same way as beef ribs, except that they are not scored. I would also suggest substituting cider vinegar for the wine vinegar in the beef marinade, as it seems to go better with the flavor of pork.

Marinate the ribs at room temperature for 1 hour or in the refrigerator for 3 hours.

Broil the ribs, keeping them far enough from the coals to prevent burning, turning often. Broiling time is about 30 minutes for spare ribs and 45 minutes for country–style ribs.

Serve with hot *tortillas*, *pico de gallo* and your favorite hot sauce.

CABRITO

Suckling Kid

Cabrito is one of the most distinctive dishes of northern Mexico. It is so popular in some areas that many restaurants, and some large ones, virtually serve nothing else. Monterrey, in the northern state of Nuevo León, is the heart of cabrito country, a rugged, mountainous region well suited to the raising of goats.

The meat of the unweaned kid, properly cooked, is considered a delicacy. In typical *cabrito* restaurants the cooking is done in the windows facing the street to tempt passersby. There you can watch as ten or more *cabritos* cook over beds of *mesquite* charcoal or coals. Usually they are prepared *al pastor* (shepherd's style). With this method, the whole, cleaned animal is spread-eagled on a spit in the shape of a cross, placed at an angle of 45-70 degrees over the bed of coals and turned about every 20-30 minutes until done (see photograph). Once done, the outside is a wonderful crisp brown and the meat is juicy and extremely tender. I would describe the taste as somewhere between lamb and chicken, on the mild or chicken side.

There are restaurants specializing in *cabrito al pastor* in the towns of Nuevo Laredo, Ciudad Acuña and Reynosa along the border with Texas, so if you find yourself in that vicinity, give yourself a treat. Because the whole kid is used, and prepared *al pastor*, this dish is rarely served in homes in Mexico. For these same reasons, it would be even more difficult to duplicate it in the United States. However, *cabrito* is now being sold, in various cuts, in the southwestern United States, particularly in Texas. In *cabrito* restaurants, it is sold by cut. Perhaps the most esteemed cut in Mexico is the *riñonada*, which is basted, as it cooks, with the flavorful fat around the kidneys. After a great deal of experience in introducing *norteamericanos* to *cabrito*, I have found that the *pierna*, or leg, is by far the most enjoyed. So, if you can find *cabrito* where you live, try to get the leg cut.

For home cooking, a number of methods are successful. I think the best one uses a water-smoker type of barbecue to smoke the *cabrito* for 1 hour per pound. Another method is to bake it in the oven at 350 degrees for 25 minutes per pound, then put it on a very hot *mesquite* or charcoal fire for about 5 minutes, turning often, until the cut is well browned and smoke–flavored. There is a restaurant in Tijuana which uses this method with great success. Almost all *cabrito* restaurants serve it in the same way. The cut of cooked meat is presented on a plate by itself, with hot corn *tortillas*, sliced onion and tomatoes, *guacamole*, *frijoles de olla* or *a la charra* and a hot sauce on the side. Alternatively, it is cut up and made into *tacos* along with the other items.

If you cannot find *cabrito*, you can make a similar dish using either a leg or shoulder of lamb prepared by one of the methods described above and served with the same accompaniments. When you visit near any of the Mexican towns above, be sure to check the yellow pages of the telephone directory for restaurants that specialize in *cabrito*, and get ready for a special treat.

CHULETAS DE PUERCO RANCHERO

Pork Chops Ranchero

This dish is made in exactly the same way as Steak Ranchero, except that 8–ounce pork chops are substituted for the steak.

MENUDO

Tripe Stew or Soup

2 lbs. beef tripe
1½ lb. calf's foot
5 cups chicken broth or water
3 chiles anchos
1 onion, chopped
1 tsp. oregano
2 Tbs. lime juice
¼ tsp. pepper
3 cloves garlic, minced
1 cup water
1 15 oz. can hominy
2 tsp. salt

CONDIMENTS
minced green onions
oregano
lime wedges
crushed chile piquín
chopped cilantro
salt

Depending on its thickness, Menudo can be either a delicious, hearty soup or a stew. It is consumed any time of the day or night in northern Mexico. Northern Mexicans can be hard drinkers and Menudo is the favorite hangover remedy after a night at the cantinas. This dish is sold by street vendors for breakfast and at all-night restaurants. Endorsing hangover cures is risky, but I will say that it does seem to work.

Menudo is made of honeycomb beef tripe, which is the lining of the cow's stomach, and a calf's foot. This may not sound very appetizing, but when it is properly cooked and seasoned even the most squeamish find it delicious. So universal is its appeal that Texas and other parts of the Southwest hold big Menudo "cookoffs." While tripe is universally available, and most Southwest supermarkets carry frozen calves' feet, the latter may prove difficult to find elsewhere. While it is an important ingredient for the flavor and final texture of the dish, it is better to cook Menudo without it than not to cook it at all.

If frozen, thaw the tripe and soak it for several hours or overnight in water. After soaking, which should be done also for fresh tripe, to remove unpleasant flavors, slice the tripe into bite-size pieces about ½ inch thick and place in a heavy pot or dutch oven.

Add the calf's foot and chicken broth or water and bring to a boil. Place the *chiles*, onion, oregano, lime juice, pepper, garlic and cup of water in a blender and blend for 1 minute or until puréed.

Add the chile mixture to the pot, bring to a boil, and then reduce the heat so that the soup barely simmers. Cover and cook for 4½ hours, checking often to prevent boiling, which makes the tripe tough. If too much appears to be boiling off, add more broth or water as needed. Now add the hominy, including the liquid from the can, and the salt. Cover and continue simmering for ½ hour. Serve the soup with the listed condiments, which are passed around the table and added, to taste, to the soup.

Poultry
AVES DE CORRAL

Poultry is not nearly as popular in northern Mexico as beef and sea-food. Unless the poultry dish is prepared from young chickens of superior quality, you are likely to be disappointed. Included here are the recipes for the few excellent chicken dishes that I have had in the area. The Chicken Shishkebob is, in fact, one of the best northern dishes I have ever had.

ALHAMBRES DE POLLO

Chicken Shishkabob

MARINADE

3 Tbs. garlic oil (see index)

1 Tbs. lime juice

¼ tsp. salt, or to taste

pinch cayenne

2 tsp. mild chile powder

¼ tsp. black pepper

Shishkebobs made of chicken and beef are favorites in northern Mexico, where they are called alhambres. There are many northern Mexicans of Middle East descent and it is probable that Mexican shishkebobs were developed from Arab recipes. My personal favorite is the following shishkebob, in which all the ingredients seem to blend most subtly.

Bone 3 pounds chicken breasts and cut the meat into ¾-1 inch pieces. Toss with the following marinade and marinate refrigerated for 2 hours.

    Mix all ingredients well.

SHISHKEBOBS

Thin steel or wooden shish-
    kabob skewers

4 medium tomatoes, quartered,
    or 16 cherry tomatoes

2 medium onions, cut into
    ½-inch pieces

3 large chiles poblanos; chiles
    anaheim or bell peppers may
    be substituted.

4 thick slices of bacon, cut into
    1-inch pieces

marinated chicken

Thread ingredients on the skewers in the following order: 1 piece pepper, 1 piece tomato (or 1 cherry tomato), 2 pieces onion, 1 piece bacon, 2 pieces chicken, 1 piece bacon, 2 pieces onion. Repeat until all ingredients have been threaded.

    Broil the shishkebobs over hot coals, on two sides, until they are well charred but the chicken is still moist and tender in the middle. This takes about 5-8 minutes on each side if the coals are really hot. If cooking over fire is not feasible, or a charbroiler is not available, broil in the oven 2-3 inches from the heating element for the same amount of time.

    Shishkebobs are usually served with *guacamole* and rice and/or *frijoles a la charra*.

POLLO AL CARBON

Broiled Chicken

2 chickens 3-3½ lbs. each

MARINADE
½ lb. tomatillos
1 green chile, roasted
½ tsp. whole chile piquín, or
    ½ tsp. cayenne pepper
¼ tsp. cumin
¼ tsp. black peppercorns
¼ tsp. oregano
½ tsp. salt
2 cloves garlic
pinch cinnamon
⅓ cup orange juice
2 Tbs. lime juice
¼ onion, chopped

Pollo al Carbón can be baked in the oven or charbroiled with equal success.

If broiling, cut the chickens in half lengthwise (or buy them already cut in this manner). If baking the chickens, leave whole. Rinse the chickens well in cold water.

Simmer the *tomatillos* (see Ingredients) until tender, broil the green *chile*, and put them both in a blender with the remaining marinade ingredients. Blend the marinade until smooth, about 30 seconds. Place the chicken in a large ceramic bowl, cover with the marinade and marinate, refrigerated, for at least 3 hours or overnight.

If you are broiling, set the chicken halves about 8 inches from the prepared coals. Turn and baste often with the marinade until the skin is brown and crispy and, when the chicken is pricked with a fork, the juices run clear. If baking the chickens, place them in an oven preheated to 400 degrees for 10 minutes. Reduce the heat to 350 degrees and continue to roast them, basting often with the marinade until they are well browned and, when pricked with a fork, the juices run clear.

Serve with white rice and the remaining marinade as a sauce. Serves 2-4.

POLLO EN PIPIÁN ROJO

Chicken in Red Pipián Sauce

3 chiles anchos
2 chiles de árboles or japonéses
½ cup pumpkin seeds (see index)
1½ Tbs. sesame seeds
⅓ medium onion, coarsely chopped
1 heaping Tbs. peanuts
2 heaping Tbs. almonds, blanched and slivered
1 slice toast, coarsely chopped
2½ cups chicken broth
¼ tsp. cumin
¼ tsp. oregano
1 clove garlic
3 Tbs. tomato purée
1 tsp. salt
2 tsps. mild chile powder
¼ tsp. black pepper
1 3-3½ lb. chicken, cut into serving pieces
3 Tbs. lard or cooking oil

Pipián, according to an aged, leather-covered Velasquez Dictionary, means "Indian fricassee." That bare definition hardly does justice to the following two recipes. Pipiánes are braised stews thickened with ground pumpkin seeds, nuts and other natural ingredients instead of flour. In this respect they are similar to the moles. This means of thickening, now so fashionable in the various "nouveau" cooking methods, has been used in Mexico for centuries. Pipián dishes, whether prepared as stews or enchiladas, are particularly popular in the state of Sonora.

Melt the lard or heat the oil in a heavy, deep pot or dutch oven and fry the chicken pieces, turning often, until well browned. Remove to a plate or dish. While the chicken is frying make the sauce base and sauce. In a heavy iron skillet toast separately (until fragrant but not burned) the *chiles*, sesame seeds, nuts, pumpkin seeds and cumin. When they are cool enough to handle, remove the seeds and stems from the *chiles*, reserving the seeds. Toast the *chile* seeds and put them, along with the other toasted ingredients, into the jar of a blender. Add to the blender the onion, toast, garlic, oregano and 1 cup of the chicken broth. Blend at low speed 1 minute.

Cook the sauce base in the pot or dutch oven for 1 minute over medium heat, then add the remaining chicken broth, stirring constantly.

Next, return the browned chicken pieces to the pot and add the salt, pepper, *chile* powder and tomato purée. Partially cover the pot and simmer for 20 minutes. Then simmer uncovered for 5 minutes. Remove the chicken to individual serving plates, turn the heat to medium-high and reduce the sauce until it begins to thicken, about 5 minutes.

Pour the sauce over the chicken and serve with Mexican rice. (See also Enchiladas en Pipián Rojo.)

POLLO EN PIPIÁN VERDE

Chicken in Green Pipián Sauce

1 3-3½ pound chicken, cut into serving pieces

3 Tbs. lard or cooking oil

8 oz. tomatillos, simmered until tender

3 jalapeños, broiled and seeded

½ tsp. cumin

¼ tsp. black pepper

1 tsp. oregano

½ tsp. salt

2 medium cloves garlic, minced

pinch cinnamon

¼ onion, coarsely chopped

¼ cup almonds, blanched, slivered and toasted

¼ cup pumpkin seeds, toasted

2 Tbs. sesame seeds, toasted

1 piece white bread, toasted and coarsely chopped

½ cup sour orange juice (see index)

1 cup chicken broth

As with Pollo en Pipián Rojo, this recipe is thickened by ingredients other than flour. It probably originated in the south, because the use of Seville or sour oranges (see index) is rare in the north. However, the chef at the restaurant in the Sonoran border town of Agua Prieta, where I collected this recipe, put his own distinctly northern stamp on it.

To make the sauce, place all ingredients except the chicken, lard or cooking oil and chicken broth in a blender. Blend until well chopped but not puréed.

Heat the lard or cooking oil over medium-high heat in a heavy pot or dutch oven, then brown the chicken pieces. When browned, remove the chicken to a bowl and pour off all but 1 tablespoon of the lard or oil.

Add the sauce to the pot and cook, stirring constantly, for 1 minute. Stir in the chicken broth and return the browned chicken pieces to the pot. Cover and simmer over low heat for 20 minutes. Remove the cover and simmer over medium heat for 5 minutes. Place the chicken on serving plates. Turn the heat to medium-high and reduce the sauce until it begins to thicken, about 5 minutes.

Pour the sauce over the chicken and serve with white or Mexican rice.

GUAJALOTE O POLLO EN MOLE

Turkey or Chicken Mole

4 chiles anchos

1 chile de árbol or japonés

⅔ cup hot water

3 whole cloves

3 peppercorns

½ stick cinnamon

1 tsp. chile ancho seeds

1½ Tbs. sesame seeds

1 clove garlic

5 whole almonds, blanched

½ corn tortilla

½ slice dry white bread

½ tsp. salt, or to taste

½ tsp. sugar

4 semi-sweet chocolate chips

1 cup chicken broth

2 Tbs. lard or cooking oil

There are all manner of legends surrounding the invention of Mole de Guajalote (turkey mole), the most popular being that it originated with a nun who, upon hearing that a clerical dignitary intended to grace the convent with his presence, threw every available ingredient into the pot along with the turkey. Whether her hands were guided by divine intervention we will never know. What we do know is that this dish comes from the southern city of Puebla and is now a Mexican classic. Sadly enough, most restaurants on this side of the Border use a ready-made commercial sauce as the base for the mole, instead of toasting and grinding the chiles and other ingredients by hand. This is like presenting a packaged French onion soup as the genuine Les Halles original!

In northern Mexico, mole sauce is used on enchiladas as often as it is served as the traditional main dish, and more often with chicken than turkey. The Mole Enchilada is one of the accompaniments to steak Tampiqueña, the premier Mexican combination plate.

Toast the *chiles* over medium heat until pliable and fragrant, taking care to avoid burning. Remove the seeds and stems from the toasted *chiles* and cover with ¾ cup of hot water.

Toast separately: the cloves, peppercorns, cinnamon, *chile* seeds, sesame seeds, garlic and almonds, and grind them in a spice or coffee grinder.

Place the *chiles* and ground spices in a blender and add the water in which the *chiles* were soaked. Fry the half *tortilla* in a little hot oil, break it into pieces and add to the blender. Toast the bread, then tear into small pieces and add to the blender.

Blend all the ingredients in the blender for about 1 minute or until they have the consistency of a smooth paste. Melt lard or heat oil in a saucepan, add the sauce from the blender, and fry over moderate heat for 5 minutes. Add the broth slowly, stirring constantly, until it is incorporated into the sauce. Simmer over low heat for 10 minutes, adding more broth if the sauce becomes too thick.

Add the sugar, salt and chocolate and stir until chocolate has just melted into the sauce.

This is the basic sauce for *enchiladas* or base for the traditional turkey or chicken *mole*. For Chicken Mole, brown in a dutch oven one 3-3½ pound cut-up fryer in 3 Tablespoons lard or cooking oil. Add the sauce base and enough broth to barely cover the chicken. Simmer covered for 45 minutes. Remove cover and simmer for an additional 15 minutes or until the sauce has thickened.

For Turkey Mole, triple the sauce base and use the procedure for Chicken Mole, substituting an 8-pound turkey. (See also Mole Enchiladas).

PALOMAS ASADAS

Broiled Dove

8 doves, cleaned and plucked
½ cup garlic oil
¼ cup lime juice
2 tsp. chile powder
½ tsp. salt
8 slices bacon (optional)

Combine the oil, lime juice, *chile* powder and salt and marinate the dove for ½ hour, refrigerated. Wrap each dove in a slice of bacon (if used) and secure with a toothpick. Broil the doves over low coals to the desired degree of doneness. My choice is medium-rare, because additional cooking makes them dry.

CODORNIZ EMPANIZADA

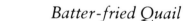

Batter-fried Quail

4-8 quail, cleaned and plucked
1 cup flour
¼ tsp. mild chile powder
¼ tsp. salt
1 egg, beaten
water
additional flour
oil for deep frying

Quail is considered a delicacy in northern Mexico and is particularly popular along the Border.

Rinse and dry the quail.

To make the batter, stir the *chile* powder and salt into the flour, then stir in the egg. Add water, stirring in slowly to prevent lumps, until the mixture has the consistency of a light pancake batter.

Heat the oil to 375 degrees.

Dip the quail in flour and shake off the excess, dip in the batter, and once again coat with flour. Deep fry quail until golden brown.

Seafood
MARISCOS

Northern Mexico's fresh seafood comes from Baja California and the Sea of Cortez, off Guaymas and Mazatlán. Red snapper, shrimp, lobster, abalone, sea bass and halibut are some of the preferred offerings. Fresh seafood is not available at all times, but it is very popular all over the north. Almost every fair-sized town has at least one *ostioneria* (oyster shop). Since oysters are rarely available, fried shrimp, fish and seafood cocktails are more often served in these small seafood cafes.

Surprisingly, the best and freshest tasting fish in the area is not found along the coast but in the state of Chihuahua. Here Boquillas and neighboring lakes and reservoirs supply daily loads of freshwater black bass to both Ciudad Juárez and Chihuahua City. Black bass is very good fried whole with only a dusting of flour or, more delicious still, broiled and served *al mojo de ajo* (with garlic sauce). If you are ever near El Paso, I recommend a detour into Juárez, just across the Border, to one of the many fine restaurants featuring this wonderful dish.

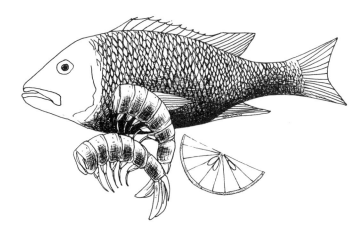

HUACHINANGO AL MOJO DE AJO

Red Snapper in Garlic Sauce

4 1½-lb. red snappers, or fresh
    water bass, cleaned and with
    the heads left on
1 cup flour mixed with 1 tsp.
    salt, ½ tsp. pepper and 1 tsp.
    paprika
oil for deep frying
¼ lb. (1 stick) butter
8 medium garlic cloves, chopped
⅓ cup cilantro, chopped and
    loosely packed (optional)
limes, halved

Seafood with garlic sauce is a dish served in many parts of Mexico. In the north it is usually made with red snapper or fresh water bass. Like many other northern dishes, it is simple to prepare and tasty eating. The fish can be either deep fried or charbroiled.

FRYING

In a heavy dutch oven or deep fat fryer, heat oil for deep frying to 350-375 degrees.

Using a fish scraper or the blade of a serrated knife, scrape as many scales as possible from the fish. Dredge one of the fish in the flour mixture, shake off the excess and, using kitchen tongs, plunge into the oil. Cook for 1-2 minutes on each side, until the fish is well browned but still moist and flakey inside. A little experimenting will yield the best timing for your particular equipment.

Place the cooked fish, on a platter covered with paper towels, in a warm oven. Repeat for the remaining fish. To prepare the sauce, melt the butter in a saucepan, add the garlic and cook over medium-high heat until the garlic is very soft and just beginning to brown. Place the fish on individual serving plates, add the *cilantro* to the sauce, if used, and spoon over the fish.

Serve with lime halves.

CHARBROILING

Brush the fish with melted butter and broil over hot coals, 5-8 minutes on each side, or until the fish begins to flake when tested with a fork. Prepare the sauce as described above. Serve with white rice, *guacamole*, a garnish made from sliced lettuce and tomatoes, lime halves, and *bolillos* with butter.

CAMARONES ASADOS

Broiled Shrimp

Broiled shrimp are prepared in several ways in Mexico. They can be marinated in elaborate marinades, or simply brushed with melted butter and lime juice during cooking. Whichever method you choose, be sure to use jumbo shrimp (10-14 to the pound), as smaller shrimp will be cooked through and dry before they are browned on the outside. For the same reason, shrimp should be cooked very close to a very hot fire. It also helps to use thin shish-kebob skewers, as this also facilitates handling the shrimp near the heat. My preferred method of broiling shrimp is simply to baste them with a mixture of melted butter, lime juice and chopped cilantro while they are broiling. However, I would also suggest you try the marinades (see index) for broiled chicken, beef or pork ribs, and chicken shishkebobs.

Marinate, for from 1 to 3 hours, approximately 6 to 8 ounces of peeled and deveined jumbo shrimp per person.

Thread the shrimp on shishkebob skewers and broil about 3 inches from very hot coals, until they are just cooked through, and not a moment longer. (Perfecting the timing may take some practice, but it is worth it: there is nothing worse than overcooked shrimp, and nothing tastier than well cooked shrimp.

To make the shrimp *al mojo de ajo* (with garlic sauce), sauté 2 chopped cloves garlic per person in 1 tablespoon butter or 1 tablespoon olive oil per person. Pour over the shrimp after they have been placed on serving plates.

Serve immediately with white rice, *bolillos* and lime wedges.

CAMARONES AL MOJO DE AJO, I

Shrimp with Garlic Sauce, I

SHRIMP

2 lbs. shrimp medium to
    medium-large (26-34
    per lb.)
flour for dredging
2 eggs
2 Tbs. olive oil
⅓ cup milk
¼ tsp. salt
¼ tsp. hot chile powder or
    cayenne pepper
bread crumbs for coating.

SAUCE

¼ cup good quality olive oil
2 Tbs. garlic, coarsely chopped

This is a favorite in the north, particularly in Baja California and Sonora. Several different excellent variations follow. You may prefer one or two, but all of them are well worth trying.

Shell and devein the shrimp, leaving the tails intact. Dredge the shrimp with the flour and shake off the excess.

Mix thoroughly the eggs, 2 tablespoons of olive oil, milk and hot pepper. Dip the shrimp in this mixture, then coat with bread crumbs. Place the coated shrimp in the refrigerator for about 1 hour before cooking.

Heat oil to approximately 375 degrees in a deep-fat fryer or in a deep, heavy skillet or dutch oven. Fry the shrimp, until golden, in 3 batches. Drain them on paper towels and place on serving plates.

Cook the garlic in the olive oil over medium-high heat until it just begins to turn golden. (If the garlic browns it will have a bitter taste.)

Serve with rice or French fries and lime wedges.

CAMARONES AL MOJO DE AJO, II

Shrimp in Garlic Sauce, II

2 lbs. medium shrimp (35-40 per lb.)
flour for dredging
½ cup good quality olive oil
¼ cup garlic, coarsely chopped
½ tsp. chile piquín, pulverized in a mortar and pestle, or substitute ½ tsp. cayenne pepper
salt to taste
lime wedges

This outstanding recipe is a very different from the breaded version. It may have originated in the Basque country in Spain, where I have had dishes very similar to this one.

Completely shell and devein the shrimp. Dredge them in the flour, being careful to shake off all the excess. (Too much flour will make the dish soggy; too little will make it lose its crispness.) To achieve the proper texture, the shrimp should be cooked in two equal batches.

Heat a heavy, deep skillet or dutch oven over the highest heat until very hot. The pan must be hot enough but not too hot, olive oil burns and catches fire at a lower heat than, for example, peanut oil. With a little experience you will find the right heat, but it is better to err on the side of safety (less heat) at first.

When the skillet is heated, quickly add 2 tablespoons oil, 1 tablespoon garlic and half of the shrimp. Stir as rapidly as possible, as for stir-frying, adding up to 2 tablespoons more oil (or enough to just keep the shrimp from sticking), 1 additional tablespoon of garlic and ¼ teaspoon of the hot pepper. Avoid overcooking. When ready, the shrimp will be lightly charred on the outside and perfectly moist and tender on the inside. Place the cooked shrimp on two serving plates and repeat the process with the remaining portion of uncooked shrimp.

Serve with rice garnished with lime wedges.

CAMARONES AL MOJO DE AJO, III

Shrimp with Garlic Sauce, III

1 lb. medium (30-35 per lb.)
    shrimp, shelled and deveined,
    with the tails left on
1 egg
1 Tbs. cooking oil
2 Tbs. milk
1 cup flour
½ tsp. salt
¼ tsp. pepper
oil for deep frying
4 Tbs. (½ stick) butter
4 medium cloves garlic, minced
limes, halved

This recipe is a particular favorite in the Sonoran seaport of Guaymas, where shrimp often are served within hours of being caught. A good cooking oil or olive oil frequently is used to make the sauce, so feel free to substitute this for the butter.

Make an egg-wash by lightly beating together the egg, 1 table-spoon oil and the milk. Mix together the flour, salt and pepper.

Heat the oil in a dutch oven or deep fat fryer to 375 degrees. Dip the shrimp into the egg-wash, then dredge in the flour. Put them in the oil, holding them by the tail for 1 second before releasing. Always use kitchen tongs, being careful to avoid splattering oil, as a severe burn could result.

When all the shrimp are cooked and arranged on serving plates, make the sauce by melting the butter in a saucepan, adding the garlic, and sautéeing until the garlic is soft and just beginning to brown.

Serve with rice and flour *tortillas* or *bolillos* and the lime halves.

LANGOSTA PUERTO NUEVO

Lobster

This dish is named for the tiny village of Puerto Nuevo, which lies between Tijuana and Ensenada in Baja California. Lobster fishermen there used to sell fresh caught lobster from their homes on the sandstone cliffs overlooking the Pacific Ocean. Then four or five fishermen's homes were converted to restaurants. Puerto Nuevo is now a village of restaurants serving lobster with frijoles, huge paper-thin tortillas (similar to those usually found in Sonora), rice and beer.

In Puerto Nuevo, lobster is usually fried in shallow pans filled with oil over gas burners. This unusual cooking method produces a marvelous taste and texture.

Split the lobster as for Langosta al Carbón. Do not overcook, or they will be dry and tough. Preheat a deep fat fryer to 350-375 degrees. Fry half of the lobster, and then the other half.

Serve with *frijoles a la charra* or *de olla*, rice, melted butter flavored with lime juice, flour *tortillas* and *salsa de chile japonés* or *piquín*.

LANGOSTA AL CARBÓN

Charbroiled Lobster

This recipe calls for langosta, which is not true lobster but a giant crawfish. In any case, it makes delicious eating. If you live on the East Coast, substitute Maine lobster. The fresher the better should be your rule.

Split the lobster in half lengthwise, using a cleaver or heavy chef's knife.

Brush the exposed flesh with melted butter, sprinkle with paprika or a mild *chile* powder and broil over hot coals, basting often with more melted butter. The flesh when ready should be well browned on the outside and just cooked on the inside, as for medium steak. Overcooking will cause it to become quite dry and disappointing in flavor and texture, particularly so with frozen lobster. Because lobster is very expensive, whether fresh or frozen, I prefer to do without unless I can get it fresh.

Serve with *frijoles a la charra* or *de olla*, corn *tortillas* and melted butter flavored with lime juice.

SOPA DE PESCADO

Fish Soup

3¾ lbs. tomatoes

4 large or 6 small tomatillos (see index)

1 large or 2 small chiles anchos

3 Tbs. olive oil

1 medium onion, chopped

3 cloves garlic, minced

1 chile poblano, seeded, peeled and chopped

2 small or 1 large zucchini, sliced in thin rounds and quartered

1 lb. white sea bass or similar fish, cut into ¾-inch pieces

½ lb. medium shrimp, shelled and deveined with the shells reserved

3 bay leaves

½ cup cilantro, chopped and loosely packed

juice of 1 lime

½ tsp. salt, or to taste

pepper, to taste

chopped coriander for garnish

Fish soups and stews are greatly enjoyed throughout Mexico, where they are looked upon as a "restorative." One version is called "Vuelva a la Vida": return to life. This variation, from Guaymas in Sonora, is delicious and very easy to prepare. Since it has the characteristics of a hearty stew, it merits inclusion as a main dish. The recipe calls for white sea bass, but any similar fish may be substituted. In inland areas, farm-raised catfish would be an excellent choice.

The soup is served with Mexican rice on the side. Diners can then add it to the soup "al gusto" (to taste), or eat it separately.

Broil the tomatoes and *tomatillos* until they are soft and their skins are charred. Remove to a blender.

Make a mild broth by simmering the reserved shrimp shells in 2½ cups water for 10 minutes. Remove the shells.

Add the *chile ancho* to the tomato mixture in the blender, blend for 1 minute and strain. This should make about 6 cups. (If not, just add more broth to the soup to make a total of 8 cups.)

Heat the olive oil in a soup kettle over medium heat. Sauté the onion, garlic and *chile poblano* until soft, but not browned. Add the zucchini and cook for one minute.

Add 6 cups of the blended, strained tomato mixture to the pot with 2 cups of the broth, for 8 cups in all. Add the bay leaf, *cilantro*, lime juice, salt and pepper. Simmer, covered, for 20 minutes.

Uncover the kettle and cook the fish for 5 minutes, with the liquid barely simmering. Add the shrimp, turn off the heat and allow to sit for 2 minutes.

Remove the bay leaves. Then, using a slotted spoon, remove the seafood and squash to individual soup bowls and top with the broth. Garnish with chopped coriander.

Serve with lime wedges and Mexican rice in side dishes, to be added to the soup as desired.

Fish Steamed in Foil

1 red snapper 4-5 lbs. or 4 1-
    1½ lb. fish, cleaned and
    whole
juice from 6 limes
½ cup olive oil
10 garlic cloves, minced
¼ cup mild chile powder
1 tsp. salt
heavy duty tin foil

This recipe is from Sonora, where you can buy fish fresh from the fishing boats when they dock. Often the fish has been caught within the last half-hour. The recipe uses any size fish from 1 pound up, and is excellent for entertaining. Although red snapper is called for, any similar fish, including catfish, may be successfully substituted.

Place the whole fish on a large double layer of foil and pour the lime juice over it. Allow to marinate for 1 hour.

Build a wood or charcoal fire (preferably on the beach). This should take 30-45 minutes.

Pour the olive oil over the fish, turning it to make sure it is well coated. Sprinkle the garlic, chile powder and salt over the fish, turning to season both sides.

Wrap the fish tightly in the 2 layers of heavy duty foil and put directly on the coals. Cook about 10 minutes on each side for the smaller fish, 20 minutes on each side for the larger one. Place the cooked fish on a serving platter and unwrap at the table.

Serve with Mexican rice, limes, *bolillos* and your favorite sauce.

LIGHT MEALS / SNACKS

ANTOJITOS

Snacks

ANTOJITOS

To most Americans "Mexican food" means one special family of foods: *antojitos*. This category includes the corn-based specialties such as *tacos, quesadillas, enchiladas, burritos,* and *tamales* and some other foods, such as *chile rellenos*. Although usually taken as snacks, they also often make up an entire meal. (For a discussion of the relationship of *antojitos* to *apertivos* and *botanas*, see the introduction to Appetizers.)

Antojitos are a unique feature of Mexican cuisine. They show most clearly the merging of the ancient Indian ingredients and cooking techniques with those of the Spanish. As is often the case with northern dishes, many of these *antojitos* were adapted from southern recipes, becoming something new in the process. The *taco al carbón*, a flour *tortilla* filled with charbroiled meat, is a good example of this.

In middle and upper class Mexican homes, a plate of *taco* meat is often kept on the kitchen table with warm *tortillas* and a sauce so that family and servants can help themselves during the day. However, poorer families more often make these items their main meal. In Mexico, even expensive restaurants usually serve some *antojitos* and there are many restaurants that specialize in them. In the Mexican yellow pages listings, you will find restaurants advertising their speciality of *"Antojitos Mexicanos."*

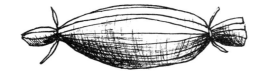

TACOS

Outside of Mexico, *tacos* are probably the best known of that country's foods, and it is one of the world's most versatile. Almost anything that is edible probably has been wrapped in a *tortilla*, and *tacos* could merit a book to themselves. In the United States, the word "taco" calls up images of the fast-food version: boiled hamburger meat in a crisp *tortilla* shell, topped with lettuce, grated cheese and some sort of red sauce. While this popular American item is not too bad, it is far different from the Mexican original.

In Mexico, *tacos* are made with soft flour *tortillas*, soft corn *tortillas*, or corn *tortillas* that have been fried medium or crisp. If flour *tortillas* are used, as they often are in northern Mexico, they should be freshly made. Most restaurants have one or two employees who do nothing but make *tortillas*, which are taken fresh from the *comal*, folded around the desired filling and served immediately. If you are not planning to serve more than eight people, prepare *tortillas* in the last few minutes. With a little practice, flour *tortillas* can be made at the rate of about 2 per minute. If *tortillas* are made in advance, they should be placed on a medium to medium–hot *comal* or griddle for about 30 seconds on each side, or until they begin to puff, before serving.

Freshly made soft corn *tortillas* also are best for *tacos*. If packaged or other than fresh home-made corn *tortillas* are used, they should be heated before serving in the same manner as flour *tortillas*.

When serving soft flour or corn *tortillas*, wrap them in a hot towel after cooking or heating and place them in a basket. This will keep them hot for some time. In Mexico, a basket of *tortillas* often is taken to the dining table with a platter containing the filling and bowls containing various sauces and condiments. Each guest then takes a warm *tortilla* and fills it with the items of his choice. This method is enjoyable and easy for large informal gatherings.

In the north, fried corn *tortillas* for *tacos* are most often cooked only to a medium crispness. This makes the *tacos* much easier to fill, as the shells are not so liable to break, and also provides a marvelous, slightly chewy texture. For either medium or crisp corn *tacos*, heat 1 inch of good cooking oil in a frying pan until it just begins to smoke. For medium–crisp *tacos*, use kitchen tongs to place a *tortilla* in the hot oil, immediately fold it as shown in the diagram, and fry for 15 to 30 seconds until the proper crispness is achieved. Experience will help you perfect the cooking time. Aim for *tortillas* that are still pliable, but a little crisp on the outside. After one or two tries, you will be making perfect *taco* shells. Remove the cooked shells to drain on paper towels.

To make crisp *tacos*, soften the *tortilla* in the hot oil for a few seconds and remove to drain on paper towels. When the *tortilla* has cooled sufficiently to permit handling, place the filling in the center and fold. Next, using kitchen tongs, hold the *taco* in its folded position in the hot oil and cook until crisp but not browned, turning frequently (see diagram).

SHREDDED MEAT FILLING FOR TACOS

1½ lbs. boneless lean beef,
  chicken, pork, turkey or
  lamb, cut into 1 inch pieces.

3 chiles anchos, stemmed and
  seeded, and left whole

3 chiles japonéses or árboles,
  stemmed and seeded

1 tsp. oregano

1 tsp. cumin

3 cloves garlic

1½ tsp. salt

¼ tsp. pepper

In northern Mexico, while many tacos are made from meat cooked al carbón and then chopped, others are made from shredded meat, whether from leftovers or meat cooked especially for the purpose. The delightful flavor and texture of these shredded meat fillings is unfortunately lost in many Mexican–American restaurants, where ground meat is often used.

Beef, chicken, pork, turkey and lamb are shredded to fill medium–crisp or crisp tacos. While the cooking process for all is the same, the seasoning combinations are endless. Here is a good, basic recipe upon which you can improvise.

Place the meat in a heavy skillet and add just enough water to cover. Add the chiles, salt and pepper. Crush the garlic, cumin and oregano to a paste in a *molcajete* or mortar and pestle and add to the skillet.

Bring the water slowly to a boil and simmer over moderately low temperature, uncovered until all the liquid has evaporated. Remove a piece of meat and check to see if it shreds easily. If the meat is not yet tender enough, add more water and continue simmering until it is properly done.

Allow the meat to cool. At this point most Mexicans shred the meat by hand, whether it was cooked especially for this purpose or whether it was meat left over from another dish. Alternatives to shredding by hand are mashing the meat in a *molcajete* or giving it a few spins in a food processor, using the steel blade.

See the section on *tacos* for instructions for making medium–crisp or crisp *tacos*.

CHORIZO

Mexican Sausage

1 lb. ground pork shoulder

5 oz. pork fat, ground

¼ cup red wine vinegar

4 chiles anchos, stemmed and
    seeded

4 medium garlic cloves

2 tsp. oregano

1 tsp. cumin

1 tsp. salt, or to taste

2 tsp. paprika

¼ tsp. ground pepper

2 tsp. chile powder

Both Spain and Mexico have many variations of the sausage called chorizo. There are probably as many recipes as there are cooks. Each village in Mexico usually has at least one sausage maker with a following who consider his chorizo to be the world's best. In northern Mexico, chorizo is sold slightly dried in a sausage casing, or in bulk without the casing. The following recipe is a rich, bulk version and is appropriate for all recipes calling for chorizo. As a high fat content is important to the making of good chorizo, pork shoulder is a choice and inexpensive cut to use.

Place the *chiles*, vinegar, garlic, oregano and cumin in a blender and blend for 1 minute into a smooth paste. If more liquid is needed, add a little water

Add the *chile* paste and the remaining ingredients to the pork and mix in a large bowl until thoroughly incorporated.

Using the fine blade, put the mixture once through a meat grinder or, using the steel blade, whirl 5 or 6 times in a food processor.

CHORIZO VERDE

Green Chorizo

1 lb. pork shoulder, ground

5 oz. pork fat, ground

¼ cup mild vinegar

4 green chiles anaheim, peeled,
   seeded and chopped

1 tsp. salt

1 Tbs. ground coriander seed

2 tsp. oregano

1 tsp. cumin

¼ tsp. black pepper

4 garlic cloves

¼ cup onion, chopped

¼ cup cilantro, loosely packed

12 drops green food coloring
   (optional)

This is a unique dish which I first sampled at La Parilla, a restaurant in Chihuahua City. I find that I now prefer it to the traditional red chorizo.

The pork should have a high fat content, so use pork shoulder or another fatty cut. However, you will still need to add extra fat, so have your butcher do this if the meat is being ground to order, or grind it yourself. (I use a food processor.)

Place all ingredients, except the pork and fat, in a blender and blend for 1 minute to a smooth paste. Add the *chile* paste to the pork and fat and mix well. Using the fine blade, put the mixture once through a meat grinder, or whirl 5 or 6 times in a food processor, using the steel blade.

Refrigerate the *chorizo* for at least 3 hours, or preferably overnight, to allow it to absorb the flavors.

Fry as you would any bulk type sausage and use for *taco* filling, alone, or scrambled with eggs.

JICAMA

Jicama is a tuberous root type vegetable that resembles a giant free from potato, basically round but with angular planes. It has a similar texture to a ripe tomato, but with a slightly sweet, fruity taste. Having achieved popularity in the United States some years ago, *jicama* is found in many grocery stores in major cities.

In northern Mexico *jicama* is usually peeled, sliced and served with chile powder or hot sauce and limes and taken as a snack. It is also an ingredient in verduras en escabeche.

FAVORITE TACOS

The following are some of the best tacos I have found in northern Mexico.

TACOS DE FAJITAS

Fajita Tacos

Make *fajitas* according to the recipe (see index). Use either the basic recipe or the one for Fajitas Encebolladas. Place slices of the charbroiled meat in flour *tortillas* and top with *guacamole, pico de gallo* and your favorite *salsa*.

TACOS DE POLLO
AL CARBON

Charbroiled Chicken Tacos

1½ lbs. boneless chicken breasts
marinade for Chicken Shishke-
    bob (see index)
flour tortillas
guacamole (see index)
½ cup green onion, minced
2 tomatoes, chopped
½ small can pickled jalapeños,
    sliced
sour cream

Marinate the chicken, refrigerated, for at least 1 hour. Broil over charcoal and slice into bite-size pieces.

Place the chicken pieces in hot *tortillas* and add the remaining ingredients. Top with a dollop of sour cream.

TIJUANA TACOS

1½ lbs. top round or chuck
    steak, thinly sliced
juice from 1 lime
salt
guacamole
one medium onion, minced
cilantro, chopped
tomatillo sauce
broiled jalapeño or serrano
    sauce
corn tortillas

These tacos are named for the border town where they are sold by street vendors. This is my favorite version.

About 10 minutes before cooking, sprinkle the lime juice and salt on the meat. Then broil it over charcoal until well done.

Slice the meat onto bite-size pieces and place on heated *tortillas*. Top with *guacamole*, onion, *cilantro* and both sauces, to taste.

TACOS DE CARNITAS

Make *carnitas* according to the recipe (see index). Place on hot flour or corn *tortillas* and top with *guacamole*, chopped green onion, and *salsa de chile ancho*.

TAQUITOS DE HARINA

Little Flour Tacos

1 lb. ground beef, lean

1 tsp. oregano

½ tsp. cumin

2 cloves garlic

2 Tbs. mild chile powder

¼ tsp. cayenne pepper, or to
  taste

⅔ cup onion, diced

12 flour tortillas, about 4 inches
  in diameter

This is one of the few Mexican recipes that uses ground meat. I first tasted it at the home of a friend who lives in a small town in the state of Coahuila. The girls in the kitchen would make 20 to 30 of these little tacos and set them on a platter in the middle of the entrance hall where anyone, including the gardeners and other servants, could stop to enjoy them. I have since had variations on the same delicious snack in many other places.

Crush the garlic, cumin and oregano together in a *molcajete* or mortar and pestle.

Heat a large, heavy skillet over medium heat and add the ground beef, breaking it up with the side of a large spoon or other suitable implement. Add the onions and the mashed garlic, oregano and cumin, chile powder and cayenne. Fry over medium heat, stirring often until the meat is well browned and the onions are soft.

Cover the pan, turn the heat very low and simmer for 20 minutes. While that is cooking, make the *tortillas* and wrap them in a thick towel to keep them warm. When the filling is done, place a heaping spoonful on each *tortilla*, fold it over and set the completed *tacos* on a warm serving plate. Serve immediately.

TACOS DE CHICHARRONES

Fried Pork Skin Tacos

In addition to serving as an appetizer, chicharrones are often steamed with various sauces and used as a filling for *tacos*. Served this way, they have a very interesting consistency and flavor. While these *tacos* are never included in cookbooks, they should be, so here are two versions.

TACOS DE CHICHARRONES EN SALSA DE TOMATILLO

1 lb. tomatillos, husked and
    rinsed
2 chiles serranos or jalapeños,
    or to taste
½ medium onion, coarsely
    chopped
2 cloves garlic
2 Tbs. cider vinegar
2 tsp. sugar
½ tsp. salt
6 cups chicharrones, broken into
    small pieces

Put the *tomatillos* in a saucepan, cover them with water and bring slowly to a boil. Then simmer gently until they are very soft, about 5-10 minutes. Place the cooked *tomatillos* in a blender jar, add the remaining ingredients, except the *chicharrones*, and blend until puréed, about 30 seconds.

Next, put the blender contents into a medium-sized cooking pot, add the *chicharrones*, stirring well, and cook, covered, over low to medium heat until the *chicharrones* are soft but not soggy. Serve with hot flour *tortillas* and sour cream.

TACOS DE CHICHARRONES EN SALSA DE TOMATE

2 Tbs. lard or oil

2 cloves garlic, minced

1 medium onion, sliced

4 tomatoes, peeled and chopped

⅓ cup salsa de chile ancho, or other hot sauce of your choice

4 cups chicharrones, broken into small pieces

Heat the lard or oil in a medium-sized cooking pot and cook the garlic and onion over medium to medium-high heat until the onion is softened but not browned.

Add the tomatoes and cook over medium-high heat for 5 minutes, stirring often. Next, add the hot sauce and chicharrones, turn the heat down, and simmer, covered, until the chicharrones are soft but not soggy.

Serve with hot flour tortillas and sour cream.

TACOS DE POLLO O GUAJOLOTE

Crisp Chicken or Turkey Tacos

2½ cups chicken or turkey meat, shredded

12 corn tortillas

2 cups lettuce or cabbage, shredded

2 medium tomatoes, seeded and chopped into small pieces

2 oz. queso cotijo or feta cheese, crumbled

hot sauce

These tacos are particular favorites in Sonora around Guaymas, and in Baja California. It takes some experience to make them properly, so I suggest preparing extra ingredients the first time to allow for a few failures.

Either a shredded meat filling (see index) or leftover meat from roast chicken or turkey may be used.

Heat 1 inch of peanut oil or another good cooking oil in a heavy skillet. Soften a *tortilla* in the oil and drain. When the *tortilla* is cool enough to handle, put 2-3 tablespoons of the shredded meat in the center.

Next, holding the *tortilla* closed with kitchen tongs, slowly lower the *taco* back into the hot oil. Cook on one side and then the other until the *taco* is just becoming crisp. Then, using the tongs, hold the *taco* slightly open at the top to allow for the later addition of the garnish. Continue to cook until completely crisp but not browned.

Remove from the oil and drain on paper towels. As you remove the *taco*, make sure as much of the oil as possible drains back into the pan. (It is difficult to give precise cooking times because of the variables, but you will soon get the hang of it.)

When all the *tacos* have been made, add some of the shredded lettuce or cabbage and chopped tomatoes to each one. This will be impossible to do if the *tacos* were not left slightly open at the top. (If they were not, just place them on a plate and cover them with the garnish and cheese. They do this as often as not in Mexico!)

Sprinkle some of the crumbled cheese on top and serve with hot sauce on the side.

ENCHILADAS

Enchiladas, like *tacos*, refers to a type of dish rather than a single recipe. It is a generic term, like cake or pie, which includes many different recipes and an almost unlimited potential for variation. An *enchilada* is a corn *tortilla* filled with meat or cheese, topped with a sauce, cheese and garnish, and then heated (except for the Sonora *enchilada*, which is somewhat different). In one common variation, the *tortillas* are folded without any filling and topped with sauce and cheese. A basic *enchilada* recipe and several variations follow.

 ## BASIC ENCHILADAS

oil for softening tortillas
corn tortillas
sauce for filling
garnish: usually cheese, onion
and, sometimes, sour cream

Place ½ to 1 inch cooking oil in a small skillet and heat it over medium to medium-high heat until a drop of water on the surface immediately sputters. Using kitchen tongs, immerse each *tortilla* for just a few seconds, then remove it to drain on paper towels. If the *tortilla* is left in the oil too long it will become hard and rubbery, and difficult to fold (and chew). A little experience will prevent this problem. In addition to softening the *tortilla*, the immersion will coat it, preventing the filling and sauce from making it soggy.

Next, place the desired amount of filling a little to one side of each *tortilla's* center, roll it up, and place it on an oven-proof serving plate. Make the remaining *enchiladas* in the same way.

When all the *enchiladas* have been rolled up, top them with the desired sauce and garnish and place them in a preheated 375 degree oven. Bake until the sauce is bubbly, about 10 minutes.

ENCHILADAS DE CHILE ANCHO

8 chiles anchos

4 cloves garlic

1 tsp. oregano

¼ cup onion

2 Tbs. olive oil, peanut oil or lard

2 bay leaves

⅓ cup tomato purée

1 tsp. salt

1 tsp. mild vinegar

2 tsp. flour, mixed with 2 Tbs. water

These enchiladas use a mild, flavorful sauce found commonly in northern Mexico, but rarely found in the United States. Make them as for cheese enchiladas, using mild cheddar cheese, and top with this sauce.

Place the *chiles*, garlic, oregano and onion in a blender, add 1 cup water, and blend for 1 minute or until the sauce is completely smooth. Add one more cup water and blend briefly.

Heat a saucepan over medium-low heat, add the oil or lard, and then the blended sauce. Add the bay leaves, tomato purée, salt and vinegar. Allow the mixture to simmer, uncovered, for 15 or 20 minutes or until thickened. Add the flour and water mixture and cook an additional 5 minutes. If, at any point, the sauce becomes too thick, add a little more water.

ENCHILADAS EN SALSA CHIPOTLE

Enchiladas in Chipotle Sauce

I came upon this enchilada recipe by chance and it is by far my favorite.

I was visiting friends in northern Coahuila and accepted an invitation to fly to a ranch some 150 miles distant. The purpose of the trip was to deliver food and other supplies for an upcoming roundup. After a smooth flight over flat desert, we climbed high over the Sierra Oriental range until we reached our destination. The ranch rests in a high valley surrounded by acre upon acre of apple and pear orchards. The main house is constructed completely of wood and stone from the ranch, except for the floor tiles which are from Saltillo. The serenity and beauty there make this one of the most wonderful places I have ever visited.

After seeing to the unloading of the provisions, we took a siesta. Upon arising, we realized that, to return before nightfall, we needed to leave very soon. In delightfully Mexican fashion, my host had not thought to worry, until just before we were to leave, that his plane was not equipped for night navigation. We strapped ourselves into the plane, only to discover that the engine was missing badly. The problem apparently was solved after an hour of tinkering, but by that time it was too late to beat the sun, which was just about to disappear over the mountains to the west. Accepting defeat, my host gave orders to ready the guest quarters and prepare dinner.

Dinner was magnificent, tenderloin steak sliced as for carne asada (see index), accompanied by the enchiladas in this recipe. When asked the name of the dish, the cook thought for a few moments, shrugged, and said, "Enchiladas de queso," or cheese enchiladas. His recipe was even less precise because, like many Mexican cooks, he cooks by feel and inspiration and, in any case, probably could not read or write. Fortunately I was able to obtain a list of the ingredients (yes, Campbell's beef broth was one. We had brought a case of it that morning). From this list I was able to recreate the recipe almost exactly.

The key ingredient of these enchiladas is the chiles for which I have named them. The chile chipotle is really the ordinary jalapeño which has been dried and smoked. They are sold dried and also canned in adobo, which is how they are used here. Their smoky flavor wonderfully enhances the charbroiled foods of northern Mexico.

THE SAUCE

4 Tbs. butter

4 Tbs. flour

1 cup Campbell's beef broth

2½ cup water, 6 canned chiles chipotle (see index), seeded and chopped

6 Tbs. of the adobo sauce from the chile can

3 garlic cloves, minced

1 tsp. oregano

1 tsp. cumin

ENCHILADAS

1 pound mild cheddar cheese, grated or shredded chicken

12 corn tortillas

½ medium onion, minced

cooking oil

sauce

Rinse, seed and chop the chiles. In a *molcajete* or mortar and pestle grind together the garlic, cumin and oregano.

Melt the butter in a medium saucepan over low heat and add the flour. Cook the roux over medium to low heat until it begins to brown and gives off a nutty fragrance. Remove the pan from the heat and add the broth a little at a time, stirring after each addition to make sure it is well incorporated. Return the pan to the heat and add the water in a slow stream, stirring constantly.

Add the garlic mixture and chiles and bring to a boil. Then reduce the heat and simmer, uncovered, stirring often until the sauce is thickened, about 30 minutes.

Heat about ½ inch cooking oil in a small skillet until it just begins to smoke. Using kitchen tongs, immerse each *tortilla* in the oil for a few seconds or just until it becomes soft and pliable. Remove to drain on paper towels.

Place about 1 ounce of the cheese and a sprinkling of onion on each *tortilla* and wrap into a cylinder. Place 3 *enchiladas* on each of 4 oven-proof dinner plates. Divide the sauce over each serving of *enchiladas* and add the remaining cheese and onion to taste.

Preheat the oven to 375 degrees. Set the plates in the oven and heat until the cheese is melted and the sauce is bubbling, about 8-10 minutes.

Serve with rice and/or refried beans, or with thin charbroiled tenderloin steak (as I had them originally).

ENCHILADAS DE QUESO

Cheese Enchiladas

ENCHILADAS

1 dozen corn tortillas

1 lb. mild cheddar cheese, grated

¾ cup onion minced

oil for softening the tortillas

SAUCE

4 Tbs. butter

4 Tbs. flour

3¼ cups mild beef broth

2 chiles ancho

2-3 chiles de árboles or
   japonéses, or to taste

2 cloves garlic

1 tsp. oregano

½ tsp. cumin

¼ cup tomato sauce (optional)

Heat the oil in a small, heavy skillet until very hot but not smoking. Using kitchen tongs, soften each *tortilla* by immersing in the oil for just a few seconds, then remove to drain on paper towels. Next, place about 1 ounce of the cheese and 1 tablespoon of the onion just off the center of each *tortilla* and wrap them tightly. Set 3 *tortillas* on each of 4 ovenproof serving plates and set aside while you make the sauce.

Toast the *chiles* over very low heat, being careful to avoid burning. Then remove their stems and seeds and soak them in hot water for about 20 minutes. Next, place the *chiles* in a blender with ½ cup of the soaking water and the garlic, oregano and cumin. Blend into a smooth paste (about 1 minute) and strain the sauce.

Next, melt the butter in a saucepan over medium heat, whisk in the flour and cook until the roux is lightly browned and gives off a nutty fragrance. Remove the pan from the heat and add about ½ cup of the broth, a little at a time, whisking constantly to prevent lumps from forming. Return the pan to the burner and continue to add the broth a little at a time, until it is fully incorporated. Then add the strained *chile* mixture and tomato sauce, if used. Bring the sauce to a boil, reduce the heat and simmer, uncovered, stirring from time to time until the sauce is thickened, about ½ hour.

Top the *enchiladas* with equal portions of the sauce and the remaining cheese and onion. Put the plates in a preheated 375 degree oven for about 10 minutes, or until the cheese is melted and the sauce bubbling.

Serve with Mexican rice and / or refried beans.

ENCHILADAS DE RES

Beef Enchiladas

1 lb. lean stew meat, cut in 1-inch chunks

5 cups water or mild beef broth

4 chiles anchos, or 4 Tbs. mild chile powder

4 medium cloves garlic, minced

½ tsp. cumin

½ tsp. oregano

2 tsp. black pepper

1 cup tomato sauce

6 oz. mild cheddar cheese, grated

½ cup onion, minced

1 dozen corn tortillas

These enchiladas are delicious when made with inexpensive stew meat, but be sure to remove all fat and gristle.

Place the meat, 1 teaspoon of the salt and water or broth in a large heavy kettle or dutch oven. Bring to a boil and simmer, covered, for 1½ hours or until the meat is very tender. Allow the meat to cool in the broth. Then remove it, reserving the broth, and shred the meat by hand or with the steel blade in a food processor.

SAUCE

Soak the *chiles* in hot water (unless using *chile* powder) for 10-15 minutes, then remove the seeds and stems and place in a blender. Add to the blender the garlic, cumin, oregano, salt, pepper and 1 cup of the reserved broth (there should be about 4 cups in all). Blend the mixture for 1 minute. If you are using *chile* powder, add it to the blender with the other ingredients.

Next, melt 4 tablespoons butter in a large heavy saucepan, add 4 tablespoons flour, and cook over medium heat, stirring constantly until the mixture begins to brown and gives off a nutty fragrance. Remove the pan from the heat and add 1 cup of the remaining broth a little at a time, stirring constantly with a spoon or wire whisk. (Make sure each addition is completely incorporated into the sauce before adding more. This ensures that the sauce does not become lumpy.) Now return the pan to the heat, set at low, and add the remaining 2 cups broth. (If you run out of broth use water.) When the broth is well incorporated, add the contents of the blender jar. Next add ⅓ cup of the shredded beef, bring the sauce to a boil, turn the heat to low, and simmer, uncovered, until it is thickened, stirring often (about 30 minutes).

ENCHILADAS

Preheat the oven to 400 degrees. Next heat ½-¾ inch oil in a small frying pan until it just begins to smoke and turn the heat to low.

Using kitchen tongs, soften each *tortilla* by immersing it for a few seconds in the hot oil. Remove and drain on paper towels. Divide the shredded beef into 12 equal portions, put one portion on each *tortilla* and sprinkle some onion onto the meat. Wrap the *enchilada* tightly, placing 3 *enchiladas* on each of 4 serving plates.

Top the *enchiladas* with a generous portion of the sauce and sprinkle the cheese and remaining onion over them. Place the plates in the preheated oven and bake for 8-10 minutes, until the cheese is completely melted and the sauce is bubbling.

ENCHILADAS SUIZAS

Swiss Enchiladas

12 corn tortillas
oil for softening tortillas
¾ lb. chicken breast, boiled and
    coarsely shredded
4 oz. Monterey jack cheese
a double recipe of tomatillo
    sauce
1 cup cream

These enchiladas, enjoyed throughout Mexico, take their name from the thick cream found in the milk-producing areas of northern Mexico. Our whipping cream is usually an "ultra pasteurized" substitute and a poor one. I suggest you make the cream as described in the section on Ingredients or, in a pinch, mix equal parts of sour cream and whipping cream.

Heat the oil until almost smoking. Using kitchen tongs, soften the *tortillas* by immersing them in the oil for just a few seconds. Remove the *tortillas* to drain on paper towels.

Place about 1 ounce of chicken on each *tortilla* and roll up into *enchiladas*.

Place 3 *enchiladas* on each of 4 ovenproof serving plates and pour ¼ cup of the cream over each one. Next, pour equal amounts of the *tomatillo* sauce over each plate of *enchiladas* and top with the remaining cheese.

Place the *enchiladas* in a preheated 375 degree oven for 10 minutes, or until the cheese is completely melted and the sauce is bubbling.

Serve with Mexican or white rice.

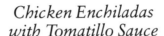

ENTOMATADAS

Chicken Enchiladas with Tomatillo Sauce

These enchiladas are made exactly like the Enchiladas Suizas except that cream is not used. I call them "Queen's Enchiladas," for reasons that will become clear.

In northern Mexican villages, it is the custom that for the yearly fiesta or fair a queen is chosen. The contestants are often selected according to the amount of money they raise for the event. At that time of year you will often be stopped, as you drive through town, by a group of young girls asking for donations *"para la reina."* (It is difficult to refuse.)

One evening at the beginning of Fiesta, I stopped to have dinner in a small restaurant in a village in Nueva León. Not having tried them before, I ordered *entomatadas*. I noticed that the rather attractive waitress was quite plainly dressed, with her hair pulled back under a scarf. When the plate arrived, about twenty minutes later, I almost fell off my chair. There she was, wearing a dress that might have belonged to Marie Antoniette, heels that must have been five inches high and a crown made of real silver, inset with multi-colored stones. Her elaborately styled hair was thick and hung below her waist.

After regaining my composure, I found out that she had been chosen Fiesta queen. The restaurant was owned by her parents and she did not seem to think it odd that she was waiting tables until literally minutes before she was due to be installed. The *entomatadas* were great!

ENCHILADAS DE PUERCO

Pork Enchiladas

1 lb. pork, diced in ½-inch pieces

3¾ cups water

6 chiles anchos, stemmed and seeded

6 medium cloves garlic

2 tsp. oregano

2 tsp. cumin

¼ cup onion, diced

2 tsp. cider vinegar

1 tsp. salt

1 cup tomato sauce

1 dozen corn tortillas

oil for softening the tortillas

1 cup sour cream

½ cup green onion, diced

This is a colorful, hearty and truly satisfying dish. The sauce is thickened naturally by cooking down the ingredients.

Place the pork and water in a saucepan and bring to a boil. Skim off the scum which rises to the top, cover, and simmer briskly for ½ hour. Remove the top from the pan and continue simmering for 10 minutes, or until only 3 cups of liquid remain. Strain half the broth into a blender and reserve the remaining half. Place the cooked pork in a bowl.

Put the *chiles*, garlic, oregano, cumin and onion into the blender and blend for 1 minute. Pour the *chile* mixture into the saucepan and add the reserved broth, vinegar, tomato sauce and salt. Bring the sauce to a boil, reduce the heat, and simmer for 10 minutes or until the mixture begins to thicken.

Heat the oil until it begins to smoke and soften the *tortillas* for a second or two, using kitchen tongs. Remove them to drain on paper towels.

Toss the reserved pork with ½ cup of the sauce. Divide into 12 equal portions. Next, make the *enchiladas* by wrapping one portion of pork blended with sauce in each of the softened *tortillas*, placing 3 each on each of 4 ovenproof plates.

Top the *enchiladas* with the sauce, then sour cream, and garnish with the diced green onions. Place the completed *enchiladas* in a 375 degree oven for about 8 minutes, or until they are very hot and the sauce is bubbling.

ENCILADAS EN MOLE

Enchiladas in Mole Sauce

These enchiladas often accompany steak Tampiqueña.

Make the sauce according to the recipe for Turkey or Chicken Mole. After adding the broth, simmer the sauce, uncovered, until it is thick enough that it will not run all over the place.

Using either shredded, boiled or leftover turkey or chicken, make *enchiladas* according to the general instructions at the beginning of this section. You can also use Monterey jack or mozzarella cheese, or a combination of both. Top the *enchiladas* with the sauce and bake on ovenproof serving plates at 350 degrees for 10 minutes.

Serve with Mexican or white rice.

ENCHILADAS EN PIPIÁN ROJO O VERDE

Enchiladas in Red or Green Pipián

These enchiladas are rarely seen on restaurant menus, but they are not to be missed.

Make the sauce by following the recipe for either Pollo en Pipián Rojo or Pollo en Pipián Verde, omitting the chicken. Next, using boiled and shredded or leftover shredded chicken meat, make *enchiladas* according to the general instructions at the beginning of this section. Top them with the sauce and bake on ovenproof serving plates for approximately 10 minutes at 350 degrees.

Serve with Mexican or white rice.

ENCHILADAS ESTILO SONORA

Enchiladas Sonora Style

masa harina, packaged

8 oz. Monterey jack or mild
cheddar cheese, grated

1 recipe sauce for enchiladas de
queso, or another sauce of
your choice

½ cup sour cream

½ cup green chiles, peeled,
seeded and diced

⅓ cup onion, minced

I have never seen enchiladas prepared this way except in Sonora. Instead of wrapping cheese in several thin corn tortillas, the cheese, sauce and garnishes are placed on a single thick tortilla. These are easy to make by following the directions on a package of masa harina. It is more difficult to make thin corn tortillas that will not crumble.

Prepare one recipe of corn *tortilla* dough according to the directions on the masa package. Make four *tortillas* about ½ inch thick and 5 inches in diameter. The easiest way to do this is to roll the dough between sheets of waxed paper.

Cook the *tortillas* on an ungreased comal at medium heat for about 5 minutes on each side, or until they are cooked through. Place one cooked *tortilla* on each of four ovenproof serving plates. In the following order, top each *tortilla* with equal amounts of the cheese, sauce, sour cream, green *chile* and onion.

Place the plates in an oven preheated to 375 degrees and bake for 10 minutes, or until the cheese is melted and the sauce begins to bubble.

ENCHILADAS FAMILIARAS

Ordinary Enchiladas

oil for softening tortillas (see
general enchilada directions)
12 corn tortillas
hot sauce
1 lb. mozzarella cheese, grated
lettuce or cabbage and tomatoes
for garnish

These enchiladas do not really have a name. However, I keep running into them in restaurants called "restaurantes familiares," or ordinary restaurants, which specialize in common or simple food at reasonable prices. They are easy to prepare and very satisfying, either served alone or with broiled meat. Use any salsa you wish. Salsa de Jalapeño or Serrano Asado, Jalapeño Cocido or Salsa de Chile Ancho are good choices.

Heat ½ to 1 inch of oil in a small, heavy skillet until it just begins to smoke and using kitchen tongs soften the *tortillas* for a second or two. Remove them to drain on paper towels.

Next, pass the *tortillas* through the sauce to coat them lightly, or rub about 1 tablespoon of sauce on each side. Place about 1 ounce of cheese on each *tortilla*, wrap loosely, and place 3 on each of 4 ovenproof serving plates. Top the *enchiladas* with more cheese and bake at 375 degrees for 10 minutes, or until the cheese is melted.

Serve with refried beans, rice and a garnish of shredded lettuce or cabbage and chopped tomatoes.

GORDITAS Y CHALUPAS

Fried Masa Snacks

2 cups masa harina

1⅓ oz. lard or vegetable
   shortening

1⅓ cups hot water

1 tsp. salt (optional)

1-1¼ cups taco filling, shredded

1 cup lettuce or cabbage,
   shredded

1 cup tomato, seeded and
   chopped

½-¾ cup cheddar cheese,
   grated

oil for deep frying

Gorditas, literally "little fats," and chalupas, which resemble the little boats indicated by their names, are favorite evening snacks. They are usually prepared and sold by street vendors and are rarely available in restaurants except by special order.

Beat the lard or shortening until it is fluffy, add the *masa*, salt, if used and hot water and knead into a ball. An easier method is to blend the water, *masa* and lard or shortening in a food processor, using the steel blade, for about 1 minute. Wrap the dough in a damp towel and set aside.

Heat about 1 inch of oil in a heavy skillet over medium–high heat.

Pinch off about 2-3 tablespoons of dough for each *gordita* and press into a 4-inch circle about ⅛ inch thick. For *chalupas*, press the same amount of dough into a boat or canoe shape about ⅛ inch thick. Pinch up the sides of the dough as you would for pizza, place on a metal spatula and slide the *gorditas* or *chalupas* into the hot oil. They will puff and brown after about 1 minute. If not, adjust the heat appropriately.

Remove the cooked shells from the oil and drain on paper towels. When all the dough has been used, top the *gorditas* or *chalupas* with the shredded *taco* filling and garnish with lettuce or cabbage, tomato and grated cheese.

Serve with the *salsa* of your choice.

FLAUTAS Y TAQUITOS

Flutes and Little Tacos

12 large or 24 small corn
    tortillas
2½ cups shredded chicken,
    beef, pork or turkey filling
    (see index)
toothpicks
oil for deep frying

SAUCE

2 medium avocados
2 tsp. pickled jalapeño, chopped
1 Tbs. liquid from the jalapeño
    jar
½ cup sour cream
Mash the avocado with the
    other ingredients and beat to
    a creamy consistency

Flautas, and their smaller cousins taquitos, are very popular snacks in northern Mexico and are frequently offered as main courses in Mexican-American restaurants. Flautas look like the flutes indicated by their name. They are made by tightly rolling one large or two small corn tortillas around the shredded meat filling, securing with a toothpick and frying in oil. Taquitos are made in the same way, except that a small, very thin tortilla is used.

In Mexico, flautas and taquitos are sold by street vendors, often cooked in advance and arranged in crispy piles on the serving counters next to bowls of sauce and condiments. In this country, they are usually served two or three to an order, often covered with a sauce made from guacamole and sour cream.

Heat the oil to 375 degrees. Dip the *tortillas* in the heated oil for just a few seconds each to soften them. Remove to paper towels to drain.

Put approximately 3 tablespoons filling on each large *tortilla* and roll as tightly as possible, securing in the center with a toothpick. If using small *tortillas*, arrange them in overlapping fashion so that the top of the lower one is in the center of the upper one (see diagram).

To cook, place 2 or 3 at a time in the hot oil with tongs and fry until crispy, about 1 minute.

Drain on paper towels and serve covered with the sauce, or serve the sauce on the side.

BURRITOS AND CHIMICHANGAS

RED CHILE BURRITOS

2 lbs. beef stew or lean pork, cut
    in ½-¾ inch cubes

water

6 chiles anchos

3 chiles japonéses or árboles

3 Tbs. cider vinegar

1 tsp. oregano

1 tsp. cumin

3 cloves garlic

1 tsp. salt

Although they are enjoyed throughout the north, burritos are most often found in the state of Sonora, and chimichangas, their fried cousins, are found almost nowhere else. Burritos are made by wrapping a filling of green or red chile, or sometimes machaca (dried beef), in a large flour tortilla. Often the chiles are mixed with refried beans and a little cheese. For a really economical meal, just beans and cheese are used. One burrito makes a great snack and two are enough for lunch. Chimichangas are burritos that have been deep-fried, which gives them a crisp, flaky texture resembling a thin pie crust.

In Sonora, burritos and chimichangas are made with huge, paper-thin flour tortillas that I have also seen in Baja California, but nowhere else in Mexico. In Arizona, across the border from Sonora, chimichangas are popular restaurant offerings. There they are usually topped either with sour cream or a sauce made with guacamole and sour cream, such as in other areas are used for flautas.

Cover the beef or pork with water in a heavy skillet and bring to a boil. Reduce the heat and simmer until the meat is tender and all the liquid has evaporated. If using beef, you may need to add additional water to achieve the desired tenderness.

Remove the seeds and stems from the *chiles* and soak them in hot water for 10 minutes. Remove the *chiles* to a blender jar, adding ½ cup of the "*chile* water." Add the remaining ingredients to the blender and blend for 1 minute.

When the meat is tender and all liquid has evaporated, add the blended sauce and simmer for 10 minutes, stirring often over low heat.

Make 8-10 large *tortillas*, about 10 inches in diameter. Spoon ½ cup *chile* on each one and fold as shown in the diagram. If left-over meat is used for the filling, it is often shredded or finely chopped, fried in lard or cooking oil until crisp, and then mixed with a favorite sauce before being wrapped in the *tortilla.*

To make *chimichangas,* deep-fry the completed *burritos* until brown and crispy. A good way to do this is to "sandwich" the *burrito* between two fryer baskets to prevent it from unwrapping during cooking.

MACHACA BURRITOS

2½ cups machaca (shredded, dried beef)

2 Tbs. lard or peanut oil

2 chiles anchos, seeded and deveined

2 cloves garlic

¼ tsp. cumin

½ tsp. oregano

¼ tsp. salt

This excellent filling may be used for burritos or chimichangas, and is also good with tacos.

Tear the *chiles* in small pieces and cover them with hot water for at least 10 minutes. Place the *chiles* in the jar of a blender and add the garlic, cumin, oregano, salt and ½ cup water. Blend for 1 minute. Add one more cup of water and blend for 30 seconds.

Heat the lard or oil over medium-low heat and add the cup of sauce. Cook, stirring constantly, for 3 minutes.

Add the *machaca* and cook for 2 minutes, stirring constantly. The mixture should be just moist but not soupy. If it is too thin continue cooking until the proper consistency is reached. If it is too dry, add more sauce. Fill and roll *burritos* as in the preceding recipe and serve, or deep-fry and serve as a *chimichanga.*

GREEN CHILE BURRITOS

This is perhaps the best of all the *burrito* fillings, especially if you use the charbroiled version. Use this filling for *burritos* or *chimichangas,* made as in the preceding recipes.

GREEN CHILI, I

2 lbs. lean meat, either chile
    (coarse) grind or cut into
    small pieces
1 medium onion, chopped
8 green chiles, peeled, seeded
    and chopped
2 Tbs. cooking oil
4 cloves garlic
½ tsp. cumin, whole
1 tsp. oregano, whole
½ tsp. salt, or to taste
1 Tbs. flour

In a heavy pot, cook the meat, onion and *chiles* in the oil over medium–high heat until the meat is browned. Add enough water to cover.

Grind together the garlic, cumin and oregano in a *molcajete* or mortar and pestle and add to the *chile*. Add the salt and simmer the *chile*, covered, until the meat is tender, about 1¾ hours. Add additional water if necessary.

Mix the flour with 3 tablespoons water and add this to the pot, stirring rapidly. Continue to cook, uncovered, until the *chile* is thickened. Serve in *burritos*, *chimichangas* or *tacos*, or over rice garnished with grated cheese.

GREEN CHILI, II

This longer process for preparing chili, using about the same ingredients, achieves superior results.

A day or two ahead, broil the meat (use chuck, about ½"-¾" thick) very slowly over *mesquite* until well done. (I usually use coals after I have cooked something else.) Allow the meat to cool and refrigerate until ready to cook.

Cut the meat into small pieces, then whirl a few times in a food processor, using the steel cutting blade, until the pieces are less than ¼ inch thick.

Soften the onion and *chiles*, using 1 tablespoon oil. Add the meat and proceed as above, but use a little less water and cook for only 30-45 minutes.

Both recipes are better if prepared a day ahead and refrigerated overnight, which allows them to thicken and absorb flavors.

QUESADILLAS

8 flour tortillas or corn tortillas,
    or 4 of each
2⅔ cup grated mozzarella
    cheese

Quesadillas make a delicious snack or appetizer and are very easy to prepare. They are made either with flour or corn tortillas, but most often with flour, and with the rich, stringy queso de Chihuahua made by the Mennonites. A good mozzarella may be substituted.

Using an ungreased *comal* or heavy skillet, heat the *tortillas*, 1 or 2 at a time, on one side over medium heat. Turn the *tortillas* and sprinkle about ⅓ cup cheese on each one.

    Continue to heat the *tortillas* until the cheese begins to melt. Then fold them (so they resemble *tacos*) and continue cooking on one side and then the other, until the cheese is melted and the *tortillas* begin to get crisp on the outside.

    Remove the cooked *quesadillas* to a warming oven, prepare the rest in the same way, and serve with your favorite sauce.

TAMALES

Tamales are made by combining ground corn, lard, water or broth and spices into a "*masa*." This is placed on a softened cornhusk, wrapped around a filling, tied and steamed. While, as with other recipes in this book, shortening may be substituted for lard, the reader is advised that it will produce less successful results for *tamales*. *Tamales* come in all sizes, shapes and types. They range from more than a foot long to finger size. They usually are wrapped in cornhusks, but in southern Mexico, particularly in the state of Chiapas, they are often wrapped in banana leaves.

    The *masa* for *tamales*, like that for corn *tortillas*, is made by soaking dried corn in water to which a small amount of dolomitic lime has been added to soften it and loosen the skin on the kernels. It is then ground to a paste and combined with broth or water, whipped lard and spices. In the south, great care is taken to remove all the skin from the corn kernels, which produces a lovely white *tamale* with a wonderful, spongy texture. This is often done in the north, as well, but there the preparation is a little more casual, and the *tamales* often have a light brown color, similar to those found in this country. Packaged *masa harina* provides a reasonably good alternative to the longer soaking and grinding method.

Tamales come in two basic varieties. The entree or snack *tamales* are made with meat or cheese and vegetable fillings. Dessert *tamales* use sweet fruit fillings.

The preparation of *tamales* is not something to be undertaken lightly. In Mexico, the whole family becomes involved in the process, often at Christmas time, when they are traditionally made and served. While it is time consuming, it can be a lot of fun to do, particularly on a rainy weekend day. Once you get the hang of it, it goes fairly quickly, as the fillings can be prepared the night before.

Tamales are often served several days (or months, if they have been frozen) after being cooked. Most Mexican cooks reheat *tamales* by steaming them, but for a much shorter period than was required during the initial cooking process. However, in the north of Mexico, they are often reheated in a skillet over low heat, or placed on a grill far enough from the coals to keep them from burning. These methods of reheating, doubtless improvised on long trail drives, produce excellent results in taste and texture.

TAMALES DE CHILE

Red Chile Tamales

FILLING

1 lb. lean pork, chopped or
   whole

4 chiles anchos, stems and seads
   removed

4 cloves garlic, minced

1 tsp. salt

½ tsp. pepper

1 tsp. cumin

MASA

1 lb. masa harina

1½ cup pork broth

½ cup chile soaking water

1 cup melted lard

½ tsp. mild chile powder

2 tsp. paprika

1½ tsp. salt

1 lb. dried cornhusks

This recipe uses pork, which is plentiful in northern Mexico, but tamales also are made with beef, chicken or turkey. A particularly delicious version uses venison.

Place the pork in a heavy pot, cover with water and simmer, covered, for 1 hour, or until the pork is tender enough to be shredded. Remove the pork from the pot, reserving the pork broth. When the pork is cool enough, shred it by hand, or whirl a few times in a food processor, using the steel blade.

While the pork is cooling, remove the seeds and stems from the *chiles*, place them in a small bowl and cover them with boiling water. Let the *chiles* soak for 20 minutes.

Toast the cumin and garlic in a small, ungreased skillet until the contents are fragrant. Avoid burning. Reserve the *chile* water and, using a *molcajete* or mortar and pestle, grind the *chiles*, garlic, cumin, salt and pepper into a paste. Mix the paste thoroughly with the shredded pork and refrigerate overnight to season.

Stir the broth and *chile* water gradually, to prevent lumping, into the *masa harina*. Add the remaining ingredients except the corn husks. The mixture should have the consisitency of a paste, spreadable but not runny. Add more liquid or *masa* as required to adjust the texture.

Soak the cornhusks for 1 hour in hot water, or until they are pliable. If cornhusks are not available, substitute a piece of white cotton cloth, as from a sheet, about 7 by 5 inches.

To assemble the *tamales*, lay a husk out flat on the work surface and cover a portion of it with the *masa*, as shown in the diagram. Next, place a heaping tablespoon of the filling in the middle of the *masa* and roll the *tamale* (as shown). Tie the ends with short lengths of string and place in a steamer.

When all the *tamales* have been rolled, bring the water in the steamer to a boil, cover, and steam the *tamales* for 1½ to 2 hours, or until they no longer stick to the husks when unrolled.

Tamales keep well and can be refrigerated or frozen and then reheated very successfully.

TAMALES DE ELOTE VERDE

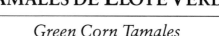

Green Corn Tamales

1 lb. masa harina

2 cups frozen corn

1 cup melted lsard

1 ⅓ cups hot water

8 oz. Monterey jack cheese

4 green or poblano chiles,
  peeled, seeded and cut in thin
  strips

corn husks, soaked for at least
  1 hour

Since the green corn required for this recipe is not readily available, I suggest using ripe corn as a good substitute.

Thaw the corn and mash it. The easiest way to do this is to give it a few whirls in a food processor fitted with a steel blade. Mix the corn into the *masa harina* and add the lard. Next, add the water to make a paste that is easy to spread but not liquid or runny.

Lay a corn husk out flat on your work surface and cover the lower right one-third with *masa* about ⅛ to ¼ inch thick. Put a strip of *chile* down the center and add a strip of cheese, about ⅛ inch thick by ¼ inch wide, on top of the *chile*. Roll the *tamale* and tie the ends with string.

Steam the *tamales* for 1½ hours, or until they no longer stick to the husks when unrolled.

NOTE: The substitution of shortening for lard is not recommended for *tamales*.

EMPANADAS

Turnovers

Empanadas are a favorite in the north. I know of one restaurant in Piedras Negras, across from Eagle Pass, Texas, that serves nothing else.

Empanadas are turnovers filled with meats and served as appetizers or entrees. They also can be filled with fruits or pumpkin pie filling and served for dessert. The following recipe is for an appetizer or entree *empanada*. To prepare dessert *empanadas*, see the recipe for coyotas, which are similar, or use this recipe and fill with any combination of fruits and nuts or pie fillings. Makes 6 *empanadas*.

DOUGH

DOUGH

2 cups all-purpose flour

½ tsp. salt

1 tsp. baking powder

½ cup shortening

1 Tbs. lard or vegetable
    shortening

1 Tbs. butter

2 eggs, beaten

water

This dough is easy to make in a food processor, using a steel blade. Put the dry ingredients into the bowl and whirl a few times. Add the shortening, lard, and butter. Process until well mixed with the flour, when a grainy consistency is achieved. Then, with the motor still running, add the eggs and just enough water to allow the dough to bind. The texture and consistency should be the same as for pie dough. If you do not have a food processor, proceed as above but cut and mix in the shortening by hand. Then add the liquids and knead for a few minutes.

Allow the dough to chill in the refrigerator for at least ½ hour. To form the *empanadas*, cut the dough into 6 pieces and shape them into balls. Roll the balls into circles of 6 to 7 inches in diameter. Place about 3 to 4 Tbs. of the filling in the center of each circle, moisten the edges, fold over and seal.

Prick the tops of the *empanadas* to allow steam to escape. Bake at 350 degrees for 25 minutes, or until lightly browned.

FILLING

FILLING

cooking oil

½ cup onion, minced

2 cloves garlic, minced

8 oz. lean hamburger

1 tsp. milde chile powder

tsp. pepper

tsp. salt

cup raisins

cup almonds, blanched and
    slivered

Heat a medium-sized frying pan over moderate heat. Sauté the onion in just enough oil to coat the bottom of the pan, for 5 minutes or until soft but not browned. Add the garlic and cook for 1 minute.

Add the hamburger in small pieces, breaking it up with a spoon to mix it well with the onion and garlic. Cook until well browned. Add the *chile* powder, pepper and salt, turn the heat very low and cover. Simmer for 10 minutes.

Add the raisins and almonds and continue to simmer, covered, for an additional 5 minutes.

Allow the filling to cool before making the *empanadas*.

TORTAS Y SINCRONIZADAS

Sandwiches

Sandwiches do not fit any category in this book, but by stretching a point they are included here. Although we may not consider sandwiches to be a Mexican food, they are greatly enjoyed as snacks and lunch foods in the north.

Tortas are made with bolillos, the crusty French type rolls, either in the classic shape or rounded. The combinations are many but here are some of the most popular:

Refried beans with cheese melted on top, sometimes with the addition of cooked *chorizo* and *guacamole*
Ham and cheese with butter or mayonnaise
Bacon, lettuce, tomato and avocado

Sincronizadas are a sort of fried *tortilla* sandwich. They are made by placing sliced ham and cheese between two flat, corn *tortillas*. The "sandwich" is then secured with toothpicks and fried in ½ - 1 inch of oil. They are usually served with *guacamole* and *salsa*.

HUEVOS RANCHEROS

Eggs Ranchero

While Huevos Rancheros do not fit into any category in this book, they are such a common breakfast or brunch item in northern Mexico that they should be included.

Huevos Rancheros are eggs which are fried, placed on heated corn *tortillas* and topped with the *ranchero* sauce for Steak Ranchero. First make the sauce and keep it warm. Next, heat the *tortillas* (usually 2 per person) on a *comal* or griddle until they have softened and begin to get crispy on the outside. Place them on serving plates.

Fry one egg, any style, for each *tortilla*. When the eggs are cooked, place them on the *tortillas*. Spoon sauce, to taste, over the eggs. Serve with refried beans, the traditional accompaniment to this dish.

DESSERTS & SWEETS

POSTRES Y DULCES

Desserts & Sweets

POSTRES Y DULCES

Dessert is not an important item on the menu in Northern Mexico. It usually consists of a small portion of flan, or some candy or fruit. Occasionally sweet or dessert tamales are served. The few recipes included here are both typical and tasty.

FLAN

❖━━━━━━━━━━━━━━━━━━━━━━━━━━━━━❖

Caramel Custard

CARAMEL SAUCE

⅔ cup sugar

cup water

CUSTARD

2 cups heavy or whipping cream

½ tsp. vanilla

4 eggs and 2 additional yolks

½ cup sugar

Even though desserts are not popular in Mexico, this is one you will find almost everywhere. While this recipe is very good when made with factory raised supermarket eggs, it is exquisite when eggs from chickens on natural feed are used.

Melt the sugar in a heavy, medium-sized skillet over moderate heat. Then add the water a little at a time, stirring constantly. Use caution, as the water will spatter when it hits the sugar. Cook the mixture for a few minutes until it is a deep caramel color. Pour the mixture into a flan pan, or a pie or loaf pan, and swirl to coat the pan until it begins to set, about 2 minutes.

To make the flan, beat the eggs and sugar until well combined. Meanwhile heat the cream until it is hot but not quite boiling. Allow it to cool for a few minutes, then beat it into the eggs and sugar, adding just a little at a time.

Pour the *flan* mixture into the caramelized pan and place it in a larger pan filled with enough warm water to come half-way up the side. Place the two pans in an oven preheated to 350 degrees.

Bake the *flan* for 45 minutes, or until the custard is set, lightly browned and a knife, when inserted, comes away clean. Remove from the oven and allow to cool. Refrigerate for at least 4 hours, or overnight.

To unmold, loosen the custard by passing a knife around the edges of the pan. Then invert it onto a serving plate.

TAMALES DULCES

Sweet Tamales

1 lb. masa harina
1 cup melted lard
2 Tbs. melted butter
1½ cup strawberry preserves
corn husks, soaked for at least 1
    hour

This dessert is a treat. Any jam or jelly, may be substituted for the strawberry preserves.

Mix together the *masa harina*, lard, butter and 1 cup of the preserves. Lay a corn husk out flat on the work surface and cover the lower right one-third with *masa*, about ⅛ to ¼ inch thick.

Spread about ½ Tbs. of the remaining preserves down the center, fold the *tamale* and tie the ends with string.

Steam the *tamales* for 1½ hours, or until they no longer stick to the husks when unrolled.

NOTE: If shortening is substituted for lard in this recipe, the results will not be as successful.

BUDIN DE LECHE O LECHE QUEMADO

Milk Pudding or Burned Milk

3 cups milk
1½ cups sugar
¼ tsp. vanilla
¼ cup pecans, diced

Leche quemado, literally "burned milk," is sold in jars throughout Mexico. It consists of milk that has been mixed with sugar and cooked into a brown paste. It is delicious but I prefer its cousin, milk pudding, which is the same milk and sugar mixture that is not cooked as long. The texture is smoother and I also prefer the flavor. Both variations make a simple but rich dessert that should be served in very small portions.

Mix the milk and sugar in a medium-sized pot, bring to a boil over medium-high heat, then turn the heat very low. The mixture should just barely simmer.

For Budin de Leche, cook, uncovered, stirring often until it has the consistency of light syrup and is still white. For Leche Quemada, continue to cook until medium brown. The milk usually begins to brown and develop a grainy texture after it has simmered for between 1 and 1½ hours. If the pudding begins to brown, remove the pot from the heat and place it in a larger one filled with cold water to stop the cooking process.

For both, add the vanilla and pecans and serve in demitasse or other very small cups.

NOTE: In Mexico this dessert is usually made with goat's milk, but cow's milk is an adequate substitute.

CAPIROTADA

Bread Pudding

12 slices French bread

⅓ cup butter, melted

4 cups water

1½ cups brown sugar

1 stick cinnamon

5 cloves

½ lb. Monterey jack cheese, grated

⅔ cup pecans, chopped

1 cup raisins

¾ cup sour cream

This is primarily a Lenten and Easter dish in Mexico. It is eaten hot, but is also good cold the next day.

Brush the bread slices with melted butter. Bake them at 350 degrees for 10 to 15 minutes, or until they are well dried but not browned. Dissolve the sugar in the water and add the cinnamon and cloves. Bring to a boil, then barely simmer, uncovered, for 20 minutes. Then remove the cinnamon and cloves.

Place 4 of the bread slices, overlapping, in a baking dish. Top with ⅓ of the raisins, cheese, nuts and sour cream. Add the next 2 layers in the same way. Pour the syrup over the top.

Place the dish in the oven and bake at 350 degrees for 20 to 30 minutes, or until it is very hot and just beginning to brown on top.

COYOTAS

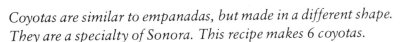

Apple-filled Pastries

2 cups all-purpose flour

tsp. salt

½ cup shortening

1 Tbs. lard

1 Tbs. butter

¼-½ cup milk

FILLING

2 green cooking apples, such as
   Granny Smith, peeled

juice of 1 lime

2 Tbs. sugar

½ tsp. cinnamon

Coyotas are similar to empanadas, but made in a different shape. They are a specialty of Sonora. This recipe makes 6 coyotas.

FILLING

Slice the apples as thinly as possible and then chop them into pieces about inch square.

Add the lime juice, sugar and cinnamon and mix well.

DOUGH

As with *empanadas*, this dough is best made in a food processor. Put the dry ingredients in the bowl and, using the steel blade, whirl a few times. Next, add the shortening, lard and butter and process until well mixed with the flour to a grainy consistency. Finally, with the motor running add just enough milk (about ¼ to ½ cup) to allow the dough to bind. The texture should be the same as for any pie dough. If you do not have a food processor, proceed as above but cut and mix the shortenings in by hand. Then add the milk and knead for a few minutes.

Allow the dough to chill in the refrigerator for at least ½ hour. Divide the dough into 12 equal pieces and shape them into balls. Roll the balls into circles, as thin as possible. They should be about 5 inches in diameter. Place enough of the filling to cover one of the circles to within 1 inch of the edge. Next, moisten the edges with water and place another dough circle on top of the covered one to make a sort of sandwich. Fold over and seal the edges. Prick the tops of the coyotas to allow steam to escape and bake at 350 degrees for 25 minutes or until lightly browned.

DULCES CON NUECES

Pecan & Sugar Candy

1 cup brown sugar
4 Tbs. butter
cup half-and-half
2 Tbs. corn syrup
2 Tbs. dark rum
1 cup pecans, chopped

This is a candy that is enjoyed in several variations throughout northern Mexico.

Butter a cookie sheet. Place all the ingredients in a small ceramic or stainless steel pan and bring to a boil over medium heat. Cook until a spoonful dropped on the buttered sheet holds together, keeping its shape and with the nuts intact. Using a large serving spoon, drop spoon-sized amounts of the candy on the sheet and allow to cool.

ARROZ CON LECHE

Rice Pudding

1 cup long grain rice
3 cups whole milk
1 cup evaporated milk
½ cup sugar
½ cup raisins
1 stick cinnamon
1 tsp. vanilla
½ Tbs. brandy
powdered cinnamon

Preheat oven to 350 degrees. Soak rice in hot water for 10 minutes. Drain and place in 2 quart pan with lid.

Add 2 cups of milk to the rice, and stir. Bring to boil, covered, over medium-high heat. As soon as the milk begins to boil, place the covered pan in the oven for 15 minutes, then remove. The milk should be completely absorbed and the rice cooked.

While the rice is in the oven, in another pan heat the remaining cup of whole milk, the evaporated milk, sugar and the cinnamon stick. Allow to barely simmer for 5 minutes. Add the raisins and brandy and simmer for an additional 10 minutes. Add the rice and continue cooking, stirring often, for 5 minutes.

Serve on individual dishes and sprinkle with powdered cinnamon.

APPENDIX

APPENDIX A
Entertaining With Northern Mexican Cuisine

Because of its simplicity, northern Mexican cooking lends itself marvelously to entertaining. The name of the most typical meal for a group, *carne asada*, denotes not only broiled beef, but a picnic or party at which broiled meat is served. A meal I had recently at the Járdines de Xochimilco restaurant in Hermosillo exemplifies the fare for such occasions. The first course consisted of a plate of *quesadillas* and small *chimichangas*. Next there was a large salad with lettuce, tomatoes and peeled green *chile* strips in a vinaigrette dressing. The main course was a plate that must have contained a kilo of mesquite-broiled tenderloin strips and another of beef ribs. Dessert was four coyotas. (This is their standard dinner for two, but would adequately serve up to six diners here.)

You may make various combinations for several festive *carne asada* dinner parties by choosing from the following items.

Appetizers:	Cacahuates Con Chile
	Verduras en Escabeche
	Roasted Pumpkin Seeds
	Tostadas with Salsas (two sauces or more)
	Fried Cornbread
	Chicharones
	Nachos
First course:	Quesadillas
	Entrees Empanadas
	Taquitos de Harina
Entree:	Carne Asada
	Fajitas
	Costillas de Res
	Cordero al Pastor
	Costillas de Puerco

Side Dishes:	Frijoles (de Olla, a la Charra or Borracho)
	Guacamole
	Pico de Gallo
	Tortillas (flour and/or corn)
	Charbroiled Green Onions
Dessert:	any of the listed desserts

This is an excellent menu for entertaining, with the cooked dishes set on platters in the middle of the table for guests to serve themselves according to individual preference. Prepare several sauces to be used with *tostadas* as an appetizer and place them on the dining table with the *guacamole*, *pico de gallo* and *tortillas*. To keep the *tortillas* warm, use covered, plastic *tortilla* warmers or wrap them in towels and serve in baskets. If necessary, *tortillas* may be heated at the last minute, in the warmer or wrapped in a towel, in the microwave oven. Avoid overheating, which makes them tough and rubbery. Serve the beans in individual bowls.

Fajitas make a good scaled-down version of the *carne asada* dinner. Bring them to the table sizzling in lime juice for a dramatic presentation. Serve everything else as for *carne asada*, using sliced *fajitas* as the only meat. Your guests may prepare their own *tacos* by placing the meat in *tortillas* and topping it with *guacamole, pico de gallo* and sauces.

Another good dish for entertaining is *enchiladas*. They can be prepared ahead of time, up to the point where the sauce, cheese and other toppings are added, then placed in the oven for the ten minutes' final cooking time. As most ovens will not accommodate more than four dinner plates, cook the *enchiladas* on platters or baking sheets and then transfer them to individual plates adding servings of Mexican rice and refried beans. Garnish the plates with shredded lettuce or cabbage tossed in a small amount of vinaigrette dressing, and stand a *tostada* upright in each serving of beans. Some *añejo* or feta cheese can be crumbled over the heated beans. To make an easy combination plate, add a steamed *tamale. Guacamole* served in fried *tostada* shells is a perfect prelude to *enchiladas*. Always provide heated *tortillas* and a hot sauce for making *tacos* with the rice, beans and garnish.

If you want to make a big hit with guests, serve a Steak Tampiqueña. But be warned that, even if you are only serving four, some experience or an extra pair of hands is necessary to make everything come together at the same time.

The foil-wrapped red snapper, or other fish, makes a tantalizing party dish that requires very little last-minute preparation. Place the fish on a platter in the middle of the table with bowls of *guacamole*, Mexican rice, *pico de gallo* and hot sauce, and *bolillos*, butter and a plate of limes. The steam rises from the fish when it is unwrapped at the table for a mouth-watering presentation. Guests then help themselves to the fish, using serving forks and spoons. Fish soup makes a perfect first course for this meal.

Carnitas is another recipe that lends itself to entertaining large groups. For a big party you can rent (or buy if you intend to do it often) a huge iron pot or cauldron in which to cook the *carnitas*. For small groups or large, begin with *nachos* and then serve the *carnitas* with flour and corn *tortillas*, several different sauces, sliced onion, and *guacamole. Enchiladas* are an excellent accompaniment to *carnitas*. Place them to the side of the *enchiladas* in some of the sauce after the latter have been heated.

APPENDIX B
Nutrition and Northern Mexican Cuisine

There is increasing and authoritative evidence that what we eat has a great impact on our health. The medical profession and professional nutritionists are urging us to reduce consumption of foods high in fat, salt, sugar and cholesterol, and recommending that we increase our intake of foods high in natural fiber and carbohydrates.

It will be obvious to the reader that some of the foods and recipes in this book are high in fat and cholesterol. T-bone steaks, ribeyes and beef ribs certainly are excluded from many diet plans. However, if such foods are used only occasionally, and in moderate portions, they should pose no problem to those whose physicians have not suggested severe dietary restrictions.

With most of the dishes included here, this question will not arise. Also, by making some simple substitutions, even those on strict diets can enjoy northern Mexican cooking without compromising the essence of the cuisine. Some of the tips and information that follow should be helpful in this regard.

Corn *tortillas* made from ground corn and water, are an ideal health food, high in fiber and carbohydrates. For flour *tortillas*, a cholesterol-free shortening may be substituted for lard and butter and the total amount of fat in the recipe cut from four tablespoons to one, reducing it to only ¼ teaspoon in one *tortilla*.

You will notice that many dishes are served with both Mexican rice and beans. Experts say that combining rice and beans creates a combination of amino acids that provides for all our protein needs. Mexican rice contains less than two teaspoons of polyunsaturated oil per serving. Although it takes longer to cook and requires more water than white rice, brown rice makes a tasty and nutritious substitution in this recipe. Simmer the brown rice in a large quantity of water for ten minutes, drain it, then proceed with the recipe, as given, adding more water as needed. The quantity of water required may vary according to the type of brown rice you are using, but you will soon discover how much you need.

Frijoles del Olla can be made without bacon or salt pork, and refried beans can be very tasty when prepared without frying. Put the cooked *Frijoles de Olla* in a food processor, add one tablespoon of oil in which two cloves of minced garlic have been gently cooked but not browned, and process.

Perhaps the most typical of all northern dishes, *Carne Asada*, is made with tenderloin which, when trimmed of all fat, has a much lower fat content than most meats. Steak *Ranchero* also can be made with tenderloin and beef stew with a diet-lean stew meat.

Many of the *antojitos* are made with cheese, which is high in both fat and cholesterol. Substitute mozzarella, which is lower in fat, for cheddar and Monterey jack, and use half the quantity called for in the recipe.

Tacos made with either soft corn *tortillas* or the lard-free flour *tortillas*, stuffed with shredded chicken or turkey and topped with any of the sauces, should present no problem to those not on a stringent diet. *Tacos al Carbón* made with chicken or very lean meat are an excellent choice for those who do not want to lose the real flavor of northern cooking while maintaining a lowered fat diet. *Entomatadas* are a fine *enchilada* option for the health conscious. Fill *burritos* with the lower fat version of refried beans, lettuce, *Pico de Gallo* and a hot sauce and add a teaspoon or two of feta cheese for an authentic and healthful "diet" dish.

INDEX

ABOUT THE AUTHOR

A longtime aficionado of Mexican cuisine and a former restaura-
teur, James Peyton raises horses on his ranch outside San Antonio,
Texas, with his wife, naturalist Andrea Peyton, whose pen-and-ink
drawings accompany the text. He has spent much of the past 20
years researching this book, which is sure to provide hours of reading
pleasure and epicurean delight for adventurous cooks everywhere.